Southern California Locals: A Railroad Enthusiast's Field Guide to Local Trains in Southern California

compiled by

Charles Freericks

BNSF Y-LAC0711 on Monaco Hill in Lawndale, CA   Charles Freericks

ISBN-13: 978-1475166781
ISBN-10: 1475166788

Table of Contents

Introduction

I compiled this list of Southern Californian local schedules so that I would have a field guide to railfan with. It consists of both my own observations and those of others who were kind enough to help. Unfortunately the railroads are constantly in flux and local jobs are dropped left and right, making any schedule perishable and subject to error at the same time. Moreover, even scheduled freight will often run hours earlier and hours later than scheduled on any given day. The information here is changing as I write this, and I encourage users to utilize this book as a sighting aid, and not as gospel. It has helped me tremendously. I hope it does the same for you. Please see the next page for instructions on how to keep your book up to date.

I would like to acknowledge the great assistance I received from a number of people, including Chris Walker, Cliff Prather, Craig Walker, David Curlee, Dave Dodds, Harry Ladd, Matt Batrynrodriguez, Peter Ely, Snufkin Rin, Virlon Smoot, and many others.

Front Cover Photo – UP LOW10 power on the Myers Team Track, Los Angeles, CA (Charles Freericks)

Rear Cover Photo – BNSF Y-LACR203 shoves into Citcom, Commerce, CA (Charles Freericks)

Organization and Accuracy

As a former colleague once told me, "There are 100 ways to do anything, and 98 of them will work."

I went back and forth about how to organize this list. In the end, I decided that the railroads would be the ultimate sort category. Yards came next, being sorted regionally. After that I used job symbols and names, which are sorted alphabetically. Industrials and short lines are also sorted regionally (beginning at Los Angeles).

Making sure that all the information was accurate has been a grueling endeavor, and to be frank, one that was not and cannot be ultimately achieved. The railroads are not interested in a book that helps railfans find locals and they do not disseminate these schedules to the public. Information can only be gathered from observation and observation at its best is an inaccurate methodology.

Use the guide as a tool, an imperfect one, but better than nothing. If you find a mistake, please e-mail me at CharlesFre@aol.com and I will correct them as possible. If a train comes five hours later than it is listed here, understand that is the nature of freight trains.

Please check out the website http://socallocalfreight.blogspot.com/. Updates are posted there from time to time so that you may update your book.

The book is designed so that you should feel comfortable writing changed information into it. It's not a keepsake. It's a tool, so as updates get posted on the website, jot them down directly into the book.

Railroad Locations and Trespass

I have included locator addresses in this work. None of these are exact, but rather what the GPS says at central spots. They won't take you to the front door of the yard office, but will take you to where the yard is so that you can find your way around.

They are not provided for anyone to use to enter railroad property with.

Pure, plain, and simple – DO NOT TRESPASS ON RAILROAD PROPERTY. This list is for your entertainment and to help you catch these trains from PUBLIC VIEWING AREAS. Railroads are very dangerous places and railroad yards are not to be accessed. There are many yards and local jobs that are not accessible to the public. They are included here because sometimes they can come out and go over grade crossings or send their power out for service. Those occasions would be the ONLY time you should try to photograph them or watch them and ONLY from public areas.

BNSF

Watson (Wilmington, CA)

(Watson – 1302 E. Lomita Blvd., Wilmington CA – some public viewing on Lomita.)

L-LAC1911   Pasha Steel Slab Train   Mon-Fri (when needed)
(On duty 1800 if there is work. Carries steel slabs imported from the Far East. The train is built by the PHL. BNSF power is brought down from Watson to Pasha, near Pier A and takes the train east on the Alameda Corridor, usually after dark. Runs at night to CSI in Fontana.)

M-WATBAR1   WatBar   Mon-Sat
(On duty 1330. Leaves Watson 1530 to 1730. Runs to Los Angeles via the Alameda Corridor. Passes Hobart Tower between 1600 and 1800. Has cars with "BORX" Borax reporting marks. Also has Styrene tanks and Propane tanks of non-odorized petroleum gas, plus a few big BNSF reefer units. Often has some autoracks loaded with Nissans.)

Y-LAC0711   Y-WAT101 Job aka 1st Watson   Mon-Fri
(On duty 0700. Heads up Harbor Sub through Torrance about 1100. Runs to the wye at El Segundo, works the Chevron refinery tracks and the lumber yard around 1230. Can be found parked somewhere between El Segundo and Lawndale while crew is at beans around 1330. Heads south again at 1400. Then works Exxon/Mobil refinery at Alcoa Yard on the way back, before returning to Watson.)

Y-LAC0712   Y-WAT102 Job aka 2nd Watson   Tue-Sat
(On duty 0630. Morning yard switcher in Watson. Handles manifest switching. Often seen with big BNSF reefer units. Only can be shot at Lomita Blvd. crossing.)

Y-LAC0722   Y-WAT202 Job aka 3rd Watson   Mon-Fri
(On duty 1430. Seen heading up the Harbor Sub from Watson as late as 1825, but usually goes out closer to 1600 and is on the way back about 1800. Works Watson yard to Alcoa and back. Switches industries at the far end of Alcoa. Can go as far north as El Segundo if there is work for it, but usually won't go north of Alcoa.)

Y-LAC0732   Y-WAT304 Job aka 4th Watson   Sun-Thu
(On duty 1559. Switches big BNSF reefers at KPAC and tank cars at Tesoro refinery adjacent to Watson Yard. Only place to see is at Lomita Blvd. crossing.)

Y-LAC0741   Y-WAT204 Relief Job   Fri-Tue
(On duty 0758. Works Watson. Also relieves the 711 job on the weekends. Relieves the 712 job on Mondays, and works afternoons on Tuesdays and Wednesdays. If in El Segundo, seems to head south about 1400. Goes to beans in El Segundo/Lawndale area just like the 711 and at the same time of day. Recently traced as T-WATSCA 00T.)

Y-LAC0742	Y-WAT404 Job	Mon-Fri
	(On duty 2230. Works Watson Yard at night and early morning.)	

Y-WAT0611	611 Shuttle	Tue-Mon

(On duty 0100. Shuttles pull and shove international stackers in and out of the Ports of Los Angeles and Long Beach. Build outbounds and yard inbounds. Transfer loaded or empty trains to and from the on-dock facilities to outlying points for later pickup including Alcoa on the Harbor Sub, ACTA 1 & 2 tracks on the Alameda Corridor, and Esperanza Yard on the San Bernardino Sub.)

Y-WAT0613	613 Shuttle	Thu-Mon
	(On duty 0631. See Y-611 Shuttle for information.)	

Y-WAT0614	614 Shuttle	Tue-Sat
	(On duty 0900. See Y-611 Shuttle for information.)	

Y-WAT0621	621 Shuttle	Fri-Tue
	(On duty 1430. See Y-611 Shuttle for information.)	

Y-WAT0622	622 Shuttle	Sun-Thu
	(On duty 1559. See Y-611 Shuttle for information.)	

Y-WAT0631	631 Shuttle	Tue-Sat
	(On duty 2359. See Y-611 Shuttle for information.)	

Y-WAT0632	632 Shuttle	Sat-Wed
	(On duty 2231. See Y-611 Shuttle for information.)	

Y-WAT0641	641 Shuttle	Sun-Thu
	(On duty 0700. See Y-611 Shuttle for information.)	

Y-WAT0651	651 Shuttle	Sat-Wed
	(On duty 0759. See Y-611 Shuttle for information.)	

Y-WAT0652	652 Shuttle	Sun-Thu
	(On duty 1700. See Y-611 Shuttle for information.)	

Y-WAT9600	Extra Shuttle	As needed
	(On duty when called. Extra two man job called when demand warrants. Spotted at Watson at 1000 on Jan 2, 2012.)	

Y-WAT9620	Extra Watson	As needed
	(On duty when called. Extra three man yard jobs called when demand warrants.)	

Pier 400 – Maersk Yard (Long Beach, CA)

(Pier 400 – 400 Pier E Ave, Long Beach, CA – no public access or viewing)

Y-THC0181   181 Job, Pier 400 APM Job   Sun-Thu
(On duty 1000. In-terminal contract switcher.)

Y-THC0381   381 Job , Pier 400 APM Job   Wed-Sun
(On duty 2100. In-terminal contract switcher.)

Y-THC0481   481 Relief Job, Pier 400 APM Job   Fri-Tue
(On duty 2100. In-terminal contract switcher.)

Hobart – Citcom – Commerce – Malabar (Vernon & Commerce, CA)

(Hobart – 3751 E. 26th Street, Vernon, CA – can watch from 26th Street, but photography mostly obstructed)

(Citcom – 6288 East 26th Street, Commerce, CA – can watch and photograph from Metrolink platform.)

(Malabar – 2504 East 49th Street, Vernon, CA – can watch and photograph from street.)

B-LACLAC   LackLack   As needed
(On duty when needed. The B-LACLAC has a B-baretable symbol whether it is carrying loads or empties. It's an extra job called to do whatever the Hobart trainmaster needs it to do – work the yard, spot carload industries, or move empty pigs or doublestacks to or from River Yard, 1st Street Yard, Commerce RIP tracks, Pico Yard, Dale Street in Buena Park, or Basta, the "Ball Park," west of Fullerton.)

M-LACBAR1   LackBar   Mon-Fri
(On duty 2000. Train is pre-assembled by LAJ crew and parked in Bell Yard at an inaccessible spot behind the National Guard Amory. Depart Bell Yard at 2100 with power from the last BARLAC. Test the FRED with a short run on the UP San Pedro Sub to Hobart. Enter CP Riddle, lined onto Main 3 at W. Hobart. Depart CP Riddle – between 2100 and 2350. Arrive and depart from La Mirada for a pickup between 2300 and 0100. The train then heads up the Cajon Sub to Barstow.)

Y-LAC0110   Citcom Job   Mon-Fri
(On duty 0631. Switches Citcom Yard, putting together stack trains. When not working, power can often be founded across the street from Commerce Platforms, parked on the C-Yard Lead. Works mornings and mid-day.)

Y-LAC0112   Malabar Switcher   Mon–Fri

(On duty at 0632. Power is kept at Malabar and rarely changes. Job is responsible for four industries, Ancon Transportation, off the Vernon Team east of the yard, Exxon Mobil, to the north, Darling International, just before the Harbor Sub joins the San Bernardino Sub, and Air Products, off Main 4 at the bottom of the Redondo Flyover. Usually done before 1330.)

Y-LAC0113   113 Job   Tue-Sat

(On duty at 0634. Works Hobart Yard switch duties or pulls baretables from 1st Street yard, lugging them back to Hobart to re-spot them on one of the buggie or loading tracks.)

Y-LAC0114   114 Job   Wed-Sun

(On duty 0758. Day shift, three man crew, normal switcher in Hobart. Has been spotted working the yard mid-morning.)

Y-LAC0211   211 Job   Sun-Thu

(On duty 1432. Works Hobart ramp or shuttles baretables to and from BNSF's 1st Street Yard. Uses a 60' flatcar as a shoving platform for shoving the long cuts of cars out of Hobart, over the flyover, and down into 1st St. Yard. They shove into the yard because there is no runaround at the north end due to Gold Line construction.)

Y-LAC0212   212 Job   Thu-Mon

(On duty 1433. Hobart Switch Job.)

Y-LAC0213   213 Job   Tue-Sat

(On duty 1559. Hobart Switch Job.)

Y-LAC0311   311 Job   Tue-Sat

(On duty 2230. Hobart Switch Job.)

Y-LAC0312   312 Job   Sun-Thu

(On duty 2231. Hobart Switch Job.)

Y-LAC0313   313 Job   Mon-Fri

(On duty 2233. Hobart Switch Job.)

Y-LAC0314   314 Job   Sat-Wed

(On duty 2357. Hobart Switch Job.)

Y-LAC2012   201 Job RCO aka Rip Job   Mon-Fri

(On duty 1556. Starts at Commerce Yard using the single unit left at Lever Brothers. Switches out the RIP tracks behind Commerce Diesel Service, and then shoves west to Hobart with the good orders and inbound Amvacs. It grabs more bad orders out of Hobart and pulls those back to Lever Brothers. They can also spot or pull Unisource when requested.)

Y-LAC2042   204 Job RCO aka Yard Hopper   Mon-Fri
(On duty 1557. Yard hops between Malabar Yard, Lever Brothers Yard, and the LAJ. Gathers Barstow cars left by the 112 Malabar job, bad-orders, Unisource, and Amvac cars, and then heads to Commerce to drop the bad orders, Unisource, and Amvacs, while gathering more Barstow cars from the RIPs or pulled from the two local industries. Heads to the LAJ between 1800 and 2200 to drop the Barstow cars for the M-LACBAR. While there, it picks up LA cars and returns those Malabar. The amount of traffic, which varies wildly, determines which yard they run to first, Commerce or LAJ. Unisource is a boxcar industry just west of Diesel Service. Amvac is located within Hobart off Buggie 8 track just south of Washington Blvd. Finish between 1900 and 2300.)

Y-LACR101   RCO-101   Sat-Wed
(On duty 0633. Works Hobart Yard. Two man crew operates with a remote equipped loco consist. The crew wears blue remote belt packs, and they lack an engineer, even though one of the conductors may be sitting in the engineer's seat at any time.)

Y-LACR102   RCO-102   Fri-Tue
(On duty 0759. Works Hobart Yard. Two man crew operates with a remote equipped loco consist. The crew wears blue remote belt packs, and they lack an engineer, even though one of the conductors may be sitting in the engineer's seat at any time.)

Y-LACR105   YLAC4105 RCO   Thu-Mon
(On duty 0635. Hobart switcher can often be seen shoving baretables into 1st Street – as part of the early week job to clear out Hobart for incoming.)

Y-LACR202   RCO-202   Sat-Wed
(On duty 1430. Hobart RCO switcher.)

Y-LACR203   RCO-203 aka Citcom Job   Fri-Tue
(On duty 1558 – Runs between Citcom and the C-Lead. Often works at the crossing over Bandini shoving back into Citcom.)

Y-LACR205   RCO- 205   Mon-Fri
(On duty 1435 – Primarily works Citcom (the old Autoveyor Yard). Builds nightly Q-LACCHI train out of CITCOM. Utility Engineer assisted.)

Y-LACR301   YLAC3012 RCO   Wed-Sun
(On duty 2232. Hobart RCO Switcher.)

Y-LACR302   YLAC3022 RCO   Fri-Tue
(On duty 2358 – Hobart RCO Switcher. Utility Engineer assisted.)

Y-LACR305   RCO-305   Mon-Fri
(On duty 2235. Hobart RCO Switcher.)

Y-LAC9900   Extra Job   As needed
(On duty when called. Extra conventional yard job called when demand warrants.)

La Mirada

(La Mirada – 14471 Macaw Street, La Mirada, CA – slightly obstructed view from street)

R-CAL0051 1st La Mirada   Mon-Fri
(On duty 0300. Switches out inbound M-BARLAC cars. Then switches industries around the yard, usually without entering the mainline, but can head onto the Olive Sub to switch out the Coast Rail transload facility by Adams Steel if needed.)

R-CAL0081 2nd La Mirada   Mon-Fri
(On duty 0700. Picks up cars in the yard, switches the Xerox lead on MWF. Switches Santa Fe Springs Mon-Fri in the afternoon between 1300 and 1700. They're easy to spot at the reconfigured Santa Fe Springs control point as no other trains use that setout.)

R-CAL0061 3rd La Mirada   Mon-Fri
(On duty 0730. Switches Kimberly Clark Spur in Fullerton after 0900, shuttling plastic pellets. Is done there by 1200. Also switches other Anaheim and north Orange County industries. Recently departed La Mirada at 0930 hours, arrived CP Orangethorpe in Fullerton at 0950 hours. Did some switching for 25 minutes. Arrived back at La Mirada at 1031 hours.)

R-CAL0071 4th La Mirada   Sun-Thu
(On duty 1700. Works La Mirada Yard. Relief switches industries outside La Mirada. Primary duty is switching Cargill at Basta and sometimes they are there two to three hours. Recently departed La Mirada at 2239 for Basta and came back at 0210.)

R-CAL0111 4th Riviera   Sun-Thu
(On duty 1800. Switches North Vail industrial spurs and South Vail industrial spurs in Commerce near the Home Depot. Transfers cars between Commerce and La Mirada and can work at Pico Rivera if needed.)

R-CAL0162 5th La Mirada   Sun-Thu
(On duty 2000 Sun-Wed. On duty in the early AM on Thu. Switches south Orange County industries and Olive Sub industries. Is responsible for the Metrolink Orange Sub south of the Riverside Freeway, SR91, which includes a juice plant and chemical companies. On Wednesday nights, head all the way to Irvine, after the last Metrolink, and then parks the power down there. Comes back early Thursday morning.)

Fontana

(Fontana – 8827 Cherry Avenue, Fontana, CA – viewable from Cherry overpass)

L-CAL0031   Pasadena Roadswitcher   Mon-Fri
(On duty 0846. After building their train, handle the Frito Lay Spur then either return to Kaiser before going west or brings its train with it down the spur and then heads west from CP Archibald usually around 10:30AM. Rarely will head up the MWD spur in La Verne. Works Pomona, between Gary and Fulton. Often stops for lunch in San Dimas or Glendora. Usually arrives westbound in Irwindale between 1300 and 1400, but can be much earlier, especially on Tuesdays, or much later. When early, waits west of brewery until 1300. Heads east approx 1530.)

L-CAL0121   Kaiser Hauler (eastbound)   Daily
M-KAIBAR
(On duty about 1700. Runs as a daily hauler from Fontana to Barstow hauling lots of steel coil cars and empty gondolas for scrap metal. Have seen going through San Bernardino as early as 0900 and as late as 1800. This is the only manifest that regularly uses the flyover from the Second District to San Bernardino. Traces as M-KAIBAR.)

L-LAC1931   Pasha Slab Train (empty)   Mon-Fri
(On duty 1900. Carries empty slab cars to Pasha in Wilmington. Won't run if there isn't a need. Has been seen heading through Colton as late as 0800, so on duty times may vary considerably.)

R-CAL1011   1st Kaiser   Sun-Thu
(On duty 0631. Switches Fontana Yard and points near there including the Muscat Spur. Territory is between CP Locust and CP Rochester on Metrolink San Gabriel Sub.)

R-CAL2011   2nd Kaiser   Mon-Fri
(On duty 0500. Switches the industrial spurs in Etiwanda and Cucamonga on Metrolink San Gabriel Sub during the day along with the Kaiser Spur to Budway and California Steel. Budway is where the U PITKAI is unloaded.)

R-CAL3011   3rd Kaiser   Sun-Thu
(On duty 1800. Switches industries in Rialto, Cucamonga, Fontana, and Etiwanda.)

R-CAL4011   4th Kaiser   Unknown
(On duty late afternoon. Switches the Kaiser Spur, working California Steel in the early evening.. Switches the south side of the main line between Etiwanda and Cucamonga.)

R-CAL5011   5th Kaiser   Sun-Thu
(On duty 2100. Switches the north side of the main at Cucamonga including the Cucamonga Foothill Spur. Has been spotted still on the spur at dawn.)

R-CAL6011-I   RLF Kaiser RSDW (6th Kaiser)   Unknown
(On duty 1445. Relieves the 4th and 5th Kaisers.)

U-KAIPIT	Steel Coil Empties	As needed

(Called when needed. Unit train from Kaiser to Pittsburg, CA. This, and its reverse move, the U-PITKAI are the only unit steel trains that use the San Bernardino Flyover. Run as needed, with the U-PITKAI being much more common than the U-KAIPIT. Kaiser Hauler handles this traffic most days when there is not enough for a full train.)

San Bernardino

(A Yard – 1187 West 3rd Street, San Bernardino, CA – can view from Amtrak platform or from the Mt. Vernon Avenue overpass.)

(B Yard – 1748 West Rialto Avenue, San Bernardino, CA – can view from the Rialto overpass, but tight chain link fence and no sidewalk on north side.)

B-SBDSBD	Baretables	As needed

(On duty when needed. Hauls baretables to/from Irwindale on the Pasadena Sub, to/from Box Springs on the San Jac Sub, to/from anywhere on the San Bernardino Sub, to/from Verdemont on the Cajon Sub day or night. Crewed by the extra board out of San Bernardino. Monday night is a good bet to see heading to Irwindale. Mondays are known as baretable day.)

G-SBDSBD	Cargill Grain	As needed

(Runs anytime of day when needed between 0000 and the next 0000. Delivers grain loads to the local Cargill elevator in Verdemont on the Cajon Sub. Has been seen at Cargill in the late afternoon, early evening, but work sheets show it has run at almost any time.)

M-SBDBAR	Barstow Hauler	As needed

(On duty 1000? When needed? San Bernardino to Barstow hauler. Believe this train runs as an extra when needed.)

O-SBDSBD1	Hostler	Thu-Mon

(On duty 0700. Has been seen bringing engines back from Commerce Diesel on a Saturday morning.)

R-CAL0141	Corona Local	Mon-Fri

(On duty 0501, but often not seen until 0830. Crew is shuttled from San Bernardino to Corona where the power and caboose are kept. Works industries from West Corona to Casa Blanca and up to Highgrove. Does many lengthy shoves. Also works 3M Spur, which is the last remnant of the Lake Elsinore branch. The 3M plant ships roofing pellets in covered hoppers. The local heads down the spur two to three times a week. Often seen in Riverside about 1100. Usually done by 1200.)

R-CAL0151   Day San Jac   Mon-Fri
(On duty at 0800. Often spotted at Highgrove on Mondays. The morning job works as far as it can down the San Jacinto Industrial Spur, leaving the rest of the work for the night job. The crew goes on duty at San Bernardino and is vanned to wherever the previous job ended. Sometimes at San Bernardino yard, more often out on the branch. The power ties up most often at either March Field siding or the Alessandro siding, both along I-215. They will meet one of the San Bernardino jobs at Highgrove to trade trains, usually between 1000 and 1200. Sometimes, the San Bernardino power will tie up at Highgrove on the branch.)

R-CAL0161   Night San Jac   Mon-Fri
(On duty at 2000. Takes over from wherever the morning job left the train. Over the period of a week, will make a number of round trips between San Bernardino and Perris on no discernible schedule. When hours of duty are done, parks where it is and leaves its train for the morning job.)

V-SBDSDG3   San Diego Autos   Mon-Fri
(On duty approx 2300, but occasionally goes on duty as early as 1715. If there is no switcher available to put the train together, won't run that night. Ferries southbound empty autoracks that come from GM at San Bernardino. Also carries loads from westbound V trains destined to San Bernardino that had cars for San Diego. Those loads go to both Pasha and Toyota at 22nd St. Slips into Sand Diego in the middle of the night.)

Y-SBD1011   Y-SBD0101 Job aka Switch 101   Unknown
(On duty in the early morning. Morning A Yard switch engine. Builds trains in A Yard, but can go anywhere in either yard or down any local BNSF line if needed. A lot of the BNSF San Bernardino yard jobs use the road power to double over the outbound trains and do the air test on Main 1, then turn over the train to the road crew.)

Y-SBD1051   Y-SBD105 Job aka Switch 105   Unknown
(On duty in the early morning. Morning A Yard switch engine. Builds trains in A Yard, but can go anywhere in either yard or down any local BNSF line if needed. See Y-SBD1011 for more info.)

Y-SBD2022   Y-SBD0202 Job aka Switch 202   Unknown
(On duty in the afternoon. Afternoon B Yard switcher. Can also work in A Yard if needed. Can do Redlands Loop work if needed. Have seen shoving a string of TOFC cars in A Yard on a Saturday afternoon. See Y-SBD1011 for more info.)

Y-SBD2031   Y-SBD203 Job aka Switch 203   Unknown
(On duty in the afternoon. Afternoon A Yard switch engine. Builds trains in A Yard, but can go anywhere in either yard or down any local BNSF line if needed. See Y-SBD1011 for more info.)

Y-SBD2041   Y-SBD204Job aka Switch 204   Unknown
(On duty in the afternoon. Afternoon A Yard switch engine. Builds trains in A Yard, but can go anywhere in either yard or down any local BNSF line if needed. Have heard working B Yard on a Saturday afternoon. See Y-SBD1011 for more info.)

Y-SBD2051   Y-SBD205 Job aka Switch 205   Unknown
(On duty in the afternoon. Afternoon A Yard switch engine. Builds trains in A Yard, but can go anywhere in either yard or down any local BNSF line if needed. Have seen building an autotrain with road power on a Sunday afternoon. See Y-SBD1011 for more info.)

Y-SBD3021   Y-SBD301 Job aka Switch 301   Unknown
(On duty at night. Switches B Yard, but can go anywhere in either yard if needed. Have worksheet showing it running through San Bernardino at 0215. Reportedly can work as the Redlands Local. See Y-SBD1011 for more info.)

Y-SBD3022   Y-SBD302 Job aka Switch 302   Unknown
(On duty at night. Switches B Yard, but can go anywhere in either yard if needed. Have worksheet showing it running through San Bernardino at 0415. Reportedly can work as the Redlands Local. See Y-SBD1011 for more info.)

Y-SBD3041   Y-SBD304 Job aka Switch 304   Unknown
(On duty at night. Midnight A Yard switch engine. Builds trains in A Yard, but can go anywhere in either yard or down any local BNSF line if needed. Might be the job that switches Kay Tee in Rialto. See Y-SBD1011 for more info.)

Y-SBD3051   Y-SBD305 Job aka Switch 305   Unknown
(On duty at night. Midnight A Yard switch engine. Builds trains in A Yard, but can go anywhere in either yard or down any local BNSF line if needed. Might be the job that switches Kay Tee in Rialto. See Y-SBD1011 for more info.)

Y-SBD4021   Y-SBD402 Job aka Switch 402   Unknown
(On duty time unknown. B Yard Relief Job. See Y-SBD1011 for more info.)

Y-SBD4031   Y-SBD403 Job aka Switch 403   Unknown
(On duty time unknown. A Yard Relief Job. See Y-SBD1011 for more info.)

Y-SBD4041   Y-SBD404 Job or aka Switch 404   Unknown
(On duty time unknown. B Yard Relief Job. Has been spotted pulling and shoving autoracks at Gonzalez in Colton on a Sunday morning at 1000. See Y-SBD1011 for more info.)

Y-SBDR202   RCO 202 Job   Unknown
(On duty around 1530. Afternoon radio control job, assigned to B Yard.)

Y-SBDR205   RCO205 Job   Sun-Thu
(On duty 1530. Works as the Redlands Local, switching the remaining active portion of the Redlands Branch. The furthest east they go is when they take tank cars of resin for chipboard manufacture to just west of Tippecanoe in San Bernardino. They might also run to Ono if needed.)

Y-SBDR302   RCO 302 Job   Unknown
(On duty at night. Midnight radio control job, assigned to B Yard. This or another unknown RCO 3 Job can work as the Redlands Local, switching the remaining active portion of the Redlands Branch. The furthest east they go is when they take tank cars of resin for chipboard manufacture to just west of Tippecanoe in San Bernardino. They might also run to Ono if needed.)

Y-SBDR402   RCO 402 Job   Unknown
(On duty time unknown. Relief job.)

Y-SBDR403   RCO 403 Job   Unknown
(Has been seen on Saturday afternoons between 1600 and 2000 working as Redlands Local, switching the remaining active portion of the Redlands Branch. The furthest east they go is when they take tank cars of resin for chipboard manufacture to just west of Tippecanoe in San Bernardino. They might also run to Ono if needed.)

Victorville

(Victorville – 16707 E Street, Victorville CA – Not very accessible and pictures are obstructed.)

L-CAL0101   Cajon Local aka 2nd Victorville   Mon-Fri
(On duty 1200. Switches the CEMEX plant in Victorville five days a week Also works the two limestone mines. Runs to Thorn and Cushenbury on the Lucerne Valley Branch if the 41 isn't able to finish.)

L-CAL0102   Barstow Turn aka 3rd Victorville   Sun-Thu
(On duty 1829. Local runs from Victorville to Barstow and back, hauling cars both ways.)

R-CAL0041   Victorville Local   Mon-Fri
(On duty 0700. Switches Victorville Yard and local industries. Heads up to Thorn and Cushenbury on the Lucerne Valley Branch about twice a week to work the Mitsubishi Cement plant below Big Bear.)

San Diego

(San Diego – Bay Front Street / Cesar E. Chavez Parkway, San Diego, CA – can photograph and watch from street.)

M-SDGBAR   Daygo   Mon-Sat
(On duty about 1800. Leaves San Diego at 1900, right after AMT 582 arrives. Makes a pick up at Stuart Mesa, adding loads of paper from Miramar. Goes through Encinitas about 2230. Makes another pick up at Porphyry grabbing the Corona Local's empties. The train has lumber, boxes, frozen food in reefers, propane, and autoracks.)

V-SDGCLO   Autoracks Eastbound   5 to 7 days a week
V-SDGALT   (On duty about 1800. Can be V-SDGCLO, V-SDGALT, or others. Follow M-SDGBAR by as little as ten minutes, but often wait for AMT 595, an hour later. Occasionally, if the inbound shipment is delayed, the switcher wasn't called, Toyota doesn't have a full release, or Passha doesn't have a full release, the train gets annulled. These are long distance trains and don't really belong in this book, but are included as they are the reverse move of V-SBDSDG.)

Y-SDG1311   San Diego Yard Switcher   Mon-Sat
(On duty at 0630 at 10th St. They run south from the yard to serve the industries between San Diego and National City. Then they pull cuts towards the convention center daily between 0800 and 1100. Tie up when done.)

Y-SDG2321   Auto Switch Engine   Mon-Sat
(On duty at 1530 at 10th St. Builds the outbound vehicle train. Take the road power to Pasha in National City at 1600. Bring the outbound train back to San Diego when the road crew is on duty – between 1800 and 2330.

Y-SDG3311   San Diego Yard Switcher   Unknown
(On duty about 0000. Performs yard duties.)

Barstow

(Barstow – 859 North 1st Avenue, Barstow, CA – can photograph and watch from many streets. Barstow is beyond the scope of this work, but these trains are included as most head into the book's territory.)

L-CAL0611   Boron Local   Mon–Fri
(On duty about 0600. Arrives in Boron around 0800, but can still be at Barstow as late as 1000. Switches the Rich Spur west of downtown. Then returns to downtown to pick up the rest of their train and the Boron caboose, a Santa Fe CE11. Train then shoves back to the main Borax plant. Return to Barstow 1400 to 1600.)

| L-CAL0111 | Kaiser Hauler (westbound) | Daily |

M-BARKAI (On duty 1400. Daily hauler from Barstow to Kaiser. Hauls manifest traffic to Fontana Yard. Have seen in late afternoon heading west at San Bernardino. Only westbound freight to take the San Bernardino flyover. Has a lot of flatcars and coil cars, loaded or empty, gondolas of scrap, lots of boxcars, lots of lumber, and a good number of grain hoppers. Traces as M-BARKAI.)

| L-CAL1161 | Cadiz Local (Cadiz Turn) | Sun-Fri |

(On duty 0600 and if they can be out of the yard by 0800 will usually make it to Cadiz by about 1130 depending on switching along the way. Swaps trains with the ARZC, turns around and heads back to Barstow. If the ARZC is late out of Parker, they will wait for them.)

| L-CAL1163 | Cadiz Extra | Sat (as needed) |

(On duty 0600. Relief job goes to Cadiz on Saturdays if there is business. If not meeting the ARZC will return to Barstow as light engines.)

| M-BARLAC1 | BarLack | Sat-Thu |

(On duty 1400. Follows the M-BARSDG out of Barstow. Makes a set out at La Mirada. Delivers into LAJ A Yard about 0200. It usually has three to six 7700 series GEVOs. Power sits in LAJ A Yard to be turned on the M-LACBAR.)

| M-BARSBD | Barstow-San Bernardino Hauler | As needed |

(On duty midday? When needed? Has been seen arriving at San Bernardino about 2100. Believe that this train is an extra, called as needed.)

| M-BARSDG | Daygo | Sun-Fri |

(On duty 1200. Runs from Barstow to San Bernardino, where it makes a large setout for the San Jacs. Then takes a short hop to Porphyry, where it sets out cars for the Corona Local. Enters the Olive Sub after SCAX 810, passing Atwood, about 1920. Does work at Stuart Mesa, usually following AMT 796 into San Diego about 2230 out of Carlsbad. Inbound loads are mostly ash for cement production in National City, paper to the Tribune, LPG to Tijuana, ethanol to Chevron, lumber to a few lumberyards – El Cajon, National City, San Ysidro and Tijuana – and grains and corn syrup to the Tecate brewer. The train also has a huge amount of autoracks. Arrive about 0300.)

| M-BARWAT1 | BarWat | Sun-Fri |

(On duty about 1500. Runs Barstow to Watson via the Alameda Corridor. Leaves Barstow mid-afternoon, gets into Watson before midnight. Often seen at Fullerton between 1900 and 2200. Cars with "BORX" Borax are a dead give-a-away. Also have Styrene tanks and a number of Propane tanks of non-odorized petroleum gas, plus a few of big BNSF refer units.)

M-BARWCL1   BarWinckle   Mon-Sat
MBAWCJ   (On duty about 1800. Handles manifest traffic from Barstow to interchange with the UP at West Colton. Most of this traffic is destined to UP customers in the LA area. It carries a lot of grain, corn syrup from ADM, and hazmat tanks. Also has a fair number of boxcars. Can carry extra tall "skyboxes" loaded with airplane parts. Usually ties down in West Colton by 0000, but can arrive as early as 2100.)

(Further Barstow info – the following general jobs work the yard –
1) Hump
2) Bowl
3) 202
4) Terminal Job
5) Herder Bleeder

Some symbols are –

        Y-BAR1022 – AM Yard Switcher
        Y-BAR1042
        Y-BAR2022,
        Y-BAR2042
        Y-BAR2062

Some manifest symbols are –

        H-BARGAL9 – Galesburg (Often combined into a two-mile long train with the BARKCK.)
        H-BARKCK9 – Kansas City
        H-BARLUB1 - Lubbock
        H-BARPAS1 -Pasco
        H-BARTUL1 - Tulsa
        H-BARVAW1 – Vancouver
        H-SLABAR9 – from Slaton
        M-BARBEL1 - Belen
        M-BARLIN1 - Lincoln
        M-BARMOD1 – Modesto/Empire
        M-BARRIC1 - Richmond

Union Pacific

4th Street Yard (Los Angeles)

(4th Street – 1115 East 1st Street, Los Angeles, CA – good views and shots from 1st St and Myers St.)

LOW10   Torrance Local   Mon-Fri
(On duty 0500. Runs south from 4th Street Yard, down the Wilmington Sub, onto the El Segundo Lead, and then onto the Torrance Lead in Gardena. Goes through Gardena about 0900. Works as far as the end of the line in Torrance, as well as the remnant of the Redondo Beach Line for Crenshaw Lumber. Only goes all the way into downtown Torrance when needed, often with engines mid-train.)

LOW20   El Segundo Local   Tue-Sat
(On duty 0659. Works 4th Street Yard, and then runs down the Wilmington Sub, onto the El Segundo Lead, going as far as Hawthorne and El Segundo on TWF. Plane parts go to Triumph in Hawthorne. El Segundo is tanks for Chevron. It reaches Slauson about 0900. Hits Hawthorne at 1000. But if not going that far, will return to 4th street by 1000. On Saturdays, does LOW10's Conoco work in Gardena.)

LATC aka Shops (Los Angeles)

(LATC – 1821 Daly Street, Los Angeles, CA – limited views from Daly, mostly cannot be accessed.)

YLZ02   LATC Hostler Job   Daily
(On duty at 1500. Finished for day 2300. Hostles power from LATC to East LA.)

YLZ14R   LATC Switch   Daily
(On duty at 0630. Finished for day at 1400. Works LATC and LA Downtown industries. Can go to Aurant to switch D&S Ingredient Transfer if needed.)

YLZ15   LATC Switch   Mon-Fri
(On duty about 0700. Finishes up around 1500. Can drag baretables to and from Aurant.)

YLZ25   LATC Switch   Daily
(On duty at 1500. Finished for day at 2300. Has been seen working as the Aurant Switch or Alhambra Switch at D&S Ingredient Transfer at Aurant Yard.)

YLZ26R   LATC Switch   Thu-Sun
(On duty 1630. Finishes by Midnight. Can drag baretables to and from Aurant.)

YLZ38R	LATC Switch	Tue-Sun

(On duty 2230. Finishes up for the day in the early AM. Can drag baretables to and from Aurant.)

YLZ41	LATC Switch	Daily

(On duty at 0000. Finishes up for the day in the early AM. Can drag baretables to and from Aurant.)

YLZ71R	Alhambra Switch	Mon-Fri

(On duty 1500, has been seen at Boca Avenue at 1600. Serves D&S Ingredient Transfer at Aurant and pulls or stores intermodal equipment in Aurant. Some days, goes down the long Mojave Granite spur that parallels Alhambra Branch in Lincoln Park to Polychemie, water treatment chemicals. Other days, picks up Polychemie cars at Soto, which were shoved up by their rail tractor.)

J-Yard (Los Angeles)

(J-Yard – 1890 East 25th Street, CA – can view and photograph from 25th Street.)

YJY66R	LAJ Transfer	Unknown

(On duty 2230. Heads out to transfer cars between J Yard and Los Angeles Junction A Yard. Leaves J Yard around 0130. Crew off duty at 0630.)

YJY68R	J-Yard Switcher	Sun, Mon, Wed

(On duty 0800 or so. Switches J-Yard. Can be observed working at 25th Street crossing. Works the Alameda Industrial Lead. This includes sugars for the Vernon Warehouse Company in the old Hamm's Brewery complex. Heads east to service City Fiber, the last remaining customer in Violet Alley, at 24th and 25th, usually on Tuesdays.)

YJY78R	3PM J-Yard Switcher	Mon, Wed, Thu, Fri

(On duty 1500. Shoves from J Yard in the late afternoon, heading across the LA River on the UP bridge. Can leave cars for LA Times on the Times Lead across Washington it also taking cars to 4th Street Yard. Delivers paper to the Los Angeles Times in the old Alameda Industrial District. This is the last customer left on the Times Lead. Also serves Hybco.)

East Yard & Spence Street (Commerce)

(Spence Street Yard/East Yard – 3632 East Washington Boulevard, Commerce CA – can view from Washington Blvd, but there is NO safe place to stop and a chain-link fence.)

ILACIR	Baretables	As needed
ILALCR	(On duty when needed. Baretable from East Yard to City of Industry, LATC, Glendale,	
ILAGLR	and Long Beach can run whenever needed. Symbol is IxxxxR – with reverse moves	
ILALBR	appropriately symboled.)	

| MLAWC | Los Angeles Hauler | Mon, Wed, Fri |

(On duty 1031 in the Weeds. This is a manifest freight hauler that runs from Los Angeles to West Colton. Has box cars and hoppers. Carries empties from various East LA Jobs back to Bloomington. Seen going through City of Industry about 1500. Arrives at West Colton about 1830.)

| SLALA | Special Switcher | As needed |

(On duty when needed. Extra jobs use this symbol.)

| YLA12 | East Yard Ramp Switch | Daily |

(On duty about 0700. Works Commerce ramp building trains. Uses road power at least part of the time.)

| YLA14 | AM East Yard Switch | Daily |
| YLA14R | | |

(On duty 0730. Works East LA and transfers to J Yard Can help out in the zones and Weeds if needed. Runs as an RCO job some days and with a full crew on other days. Builds ILALCR baretable trains. Usually finished for the day between 1200 and 1500. Power then sits alongside Washington Blvd.)

| YLA22 | East Yard Ramp Switch | Daily |

(On duty 1700. Works East LA ramp and other switching in the yard. Finishes about 2300.)

| YLA32 | East Yard Ramp Switch | Daily |

(On duty about 0000. Builds outbound trains into the early AM.)

| YLA51 | East Industry Job | Mon-Fri |

(On duty 0630. On some days it will work the Bandini Area -- the spur that heads west off the San Pedro Sub just south of Hobart along the Los Angeles River. Then on the next day it will work both The Flood near Farmer John and the Vernon Lead which is the four track spur that it shares with LAJ and which it uses to shove cars to Cargill at the end of Jewel Avenue. On MWF, leaves their entire train at the Federal, a siding along Downey near Slauson for the YLA63R to pick up. On TuTh leaves train at River Yard for YLA63R.)

| YLA61R | Ferguson Job | Sun-Fri |

(On duty about 1600. Goes to the Weeds and East L.A. North Side. Interchanges with LAJ. Calls the BNSF DS on the radio to get permission to cross over the BNSF. Serves Hickory Springs, Mission Foods, Horizon Milling, and Pacific Resource Recovery.)

| YLA63R | South Industry Job | Mon-Fri |

(On duty 1530 at Federal Siding on San Pedro Sub in Vernon on MWF and at River Yard on TuTh. Starts with train left behind by YLA51. Does the South Industry work on the north end of the sub and then brings empties back to the Weeds for the MLAWC to West Colton. Can work all the way south to Huntington Park if needed. Also switches industries in the UP River Yard and utilizes the LAJ A yard to run thru. Passes through A Yard westbound Tues and Thurs at 1600.)

YLA70R   Weeds Industrial Switcher   Mon-Fri
                (On duty 2230. Radio control job that pulls cars from 4th Street, and LATC, if needed.
                Switches and spots the Weeds at night. Serves ADM Milling, Food Express, and
                Huhtamaki Packaging.)

Gemco (Van Nuys)

(Gemco – 7724 Van Nuys Boulevard, Van Nuys, CA – can be watched and photographed from Van Nuys
Metrolink platforms – but can't see engine facility.)

LOF41   Day Bud/Northridge Switcher   Daily
                (On duty 0715. Breaks up inbound LOQ35 and LOF66 and builds the LOF65/LOF67 and
                LOF74. Covers all customers from Hewitt to Santa Susana on Metrolink's Ventura Sub,
                including General Wax, Portion Pac, DWP, Stock Building Supply, and Budweiser. Serves
                the busy Gemco team track. Can head out of yard between 0800 and 0900. Can make
                emergency Saturday run to Oxnard if hot cars missed the LOF67. Covered by the extra
                board on Sat and Sun.)

LOF42   Saugus Local   Mon-Fri
                (On duty 0600. Uses same power as LOF49. Starts by assembling their train in Gemco
                Yard. Usually departs about 0800 and heads south to Burbank Jct. From there it heads
                up the Metrolink Valley Sub, the old Saugus Line, switching industries along the way.
                Always has a caboose due to some long shoves. Observed often at CP Balboa
                northbound at 0840. Waits at Newhall at 0900 for Metrolink. Passes CP Saugus
                southbound between 1015 and 1100. It usually returns to Gemco before 1400.)

LOF49   Gemco Flyer/Night Bud   Mon-Fri
                (On duty 2000. Uses same power and caboose as LOF42. Performs night switch for
                Budweiser and serves all customers between Burbank and LA including SCAX/AMTK
                equipment deliveries/shipments, Stock Building Supply on Burbank Branch Wye and in
                Glendale, and Swaner Hardwood. Delivers spot cars to Aurant for Alhambra Switcher,
                bringing their pulls back to Gemco for the LOF74. Also serves LATC moving "home shop"
                bad-ordered intermodal equipment to Gemco for LOF74 as well as returning OK
                equipment. Brings inbound autoracks from LATC to Gemco for the LOF65/67 to deliver
                to VCY.)

LOF65   Leesdale Local   Wed
                (On duty at 1401. Delivers and pulls Oxnard and VCY traffic. Does no "short" work
                anymore. Power comes from previous LOQ35.Builds train at Gemco, then heads to
                Oxnard. Drops cars in Oxnard Yard, and heads back south to Gemco. Often seen heading
                south at Chatsworth about 1845. This train gives Ventura County Railroad and the
                Oxnard Local three-day coverage in each direction.)

LOF67   Guadalupe Turn   Mon, Thu
               (On duty 1401, but can go on duty up to two-hours early if LOF41 has their train ready.
               Air tests at Gemco, then calls the DS to enter the Metrolink Ventura Sub. Sets off cars
               for VCRY and Oxnard Local at Oxnard. Works Haywood Lumber in Goleta if needed. Also
               spots/pulls MofW equipment at Gaviota and Sacate material spurs. Heads up to
               Guadalupe with cars for Santa Maria Valley and Guadalupe Local. Arrives in Guadalupe
               between 0100 and 0200. Crew overnights at a Santa Maria motel. Power comes from
               previous LOQ35)

LOF74   Gemco Hauler   Tue-Sat
               (On duty 2000. Leaves between 2120 and 2230 with Guadalupe, Oxnard, and Gemco
               outbounds. Picks up LOW10, LOW20, LAJ, and J-Yard outbounds at 4th Street Yard about
               0130. Makes a pick up at the Weeds in East Yard. Can get up to 10K feet long. Arrives in
               West Colton about 0600.)

Mead (Wilmington/Long Beach border)

(Mead – 2284 East Anaheim Street, Wilmington CA – can see north side from street.)

LOG09R   Unknown
               (On duty 2000. Have no further information on what this job does. May very well just be
               the Watson Job, LOG10R given a different symbol on certain days.)

LOG10R   Watson Job   Tue-Sat
               (On duty 2000. Originates in Mead. Heads up to Dolores via the Long Beach Sub.
               Switches Valero Marketing Supply, BP West Coast Products, Phillips 66, and Konoike
               Pacific. Finishes up about 0330.)

LOG11R   Reyes Switcher   Mon-Fri
               (On duty 1400. Serve Compton, Rancho Dominguez, and Lynwood via the Alameda
               Corridor and the Patata Industrial Lead. Backs out of Mead onto PHL Long Beach Sub.
               Heads west onto Alameda Corridor in the late afternoon. Works along Alameda Street
               north of Dominguez on the Dolores Industrial Lead as far as CP Compton. Works the
               Reyes Spurs along the Del Amo Industrial Lead. Is on the Reyes Spurs at about 1700.)

LOG16R   7400 Zone Switcher   Mon-Fri
               (On duty 0730 but can leave earlier. Originates in Mead, running up the Manual Sub to
               put its train together. Shoves north to take the Long Beach Sub to the Wilmington Wye
               into Dolores. Works Dolores Yard and the Del Amo Industrial Park to the west of
               Dolores, including BP, Ventura Transfer, INEOS Olefins & Polymers, and PolyOne, south
               of 223rd Street. Works all the way north to Compton on the Wilmington Sub. Runs to
               Terminal Island a few times a week to switch Vopak, the only UP customer on TI.
               Returns to Mead about 1300. Also works the 7400 Zone, aka the Carson Industrial Lead,
               which parallels the 405 and crosses the Dominguez Channel in Carson near 223rd and
               Wilmington. Has been seen there as late as 1500, but is more likely in the AM.)

| LOG41R | Paramount Switcher | Mon-Sat |

(On duty 0700, departs 0900. Runs north on the Manuel and San Pedro Subs. On TWF, between 0930 and 1130, it goes to Paramount for asphalt loads from Paramount Petroleum on the Paramount Industrial Lead. On WF between 1000 and 1300, it works the Lakewood Industrial Lead for Ganahl Lumber. Also services a transloading yard at the old LASL Paramount depot, ECC California, Globe Propane, and reefers for Pacific Coast Container.)

| LOG42 | Harbor Local | Daily |

(On duty 0700. Switches out the inbound hauler, MWCLB, from Colton, and then builds and air tests the outbound hauler, MLBWC on the Manuel tracks. Does whatever switching needs to be done in Mead Yard. Delivers cars to PHL. Can run to Dolores if needed.)

| LOG44 | Mead Local | Mon-Fri |

(On duty 1800. This is actually a hauler despite its name. Carries autoracks full of imported autos, Nissan, Lexus, Toyota, asphalt tanks, dirty dirt containers on flats, and reefers. Heads to Commerce, arriving between 2000 and 2300. Is used to ferry locomotives from Dolores, ICTF, Terminal Island, etc. up to Los Angeles.)

| MLBWC | Long Beach Hauler (eastbound) | Tue-Sat |

(On duty 1600 but often leaves much earlier, even as early as 1100. Runs from Long Beach to West Colton. Grabs outbound UP cars from the Manuel passes – usually Manuel Two and Three. Arrives 0200 the next day, however, has been seen passing through Pomona at 1427.)

| OLBTN | Trona Empties | 2 to 5 times a week |

(On duty as needed. Starts at Pier G Yard. Returns empty aggregate hoppers to Searles, where they are picked up by the Trona Railroad. Usually takes Metrolink's Valley Sub, but can go via the Mojave Sub. If on Valley, tends to be an afternoon run.)

Dolores and ICTF (Carson)

(Dolores – 21847 South Alameda Street, Carson, CA – good views from Alameda, including way north at the Dolores round house near the Metro Rail Blue Line cross-over)

(ICTF – East 223rd Street, Los Angeles, CA –absolutely no access, limited views from overpass on 223rd, but not much.)

| LOI11 | ICTF Switcher | Daily |

(On duty 0500. Switches ICTF plant and support yard. Hostles power for ICTF trains. Hostles power to and from Dolores roundhouse.)

LOI13 ICTF Switcher   Daily
(On duty 0300. Builds stack trains, shoving and pulling into Dolores and ICTF. Switches ICTF plant and support yard. Hostles power for ICTF trains. Hostles power to and from Dolores roundhouse.)

LOI19 PHL Hostler Job   Daily
(On duty 1000. Hostles power for on-dock trains. Hostles power for Dolores roundhouse. Builds and air tests on-dock trains. Stages power at various on-dock facilities.)

LOI21 ICTF Switcher   Daily
(On duty 1300. Switches ICTF plant and support yard. Hostles power for ICTF trains. Hostles power to and from Dolores roundhouse.)

LOI23 4PM ICTF Switcher   Daily
(On duty 1500. Switches ICTF plant and support yard. Hostles power for ICTF trains. Hostles power to and from Dolores roundhouse.)

LOI31 ICTF Switcher   Daily
(On duty 2100. Switches ICTF plant and support yard. Hostles power for ICTF trains. Hostles power to and from Dolores roundhouse.)

LOI39 ICTF Hostler Job   Sun, Mon, Tue
(On duty 2200. Hostles power for on-dock trains. Hostles power for Dolores roundhouse. Builds and air tests on-dock trains. Stages power at various on-dock facilities.)

ODOWP Oil Cans   sked for Thursday, but runs about every other day
(On duty between 1700 and 2000, but can be any time. Empty train of three sets of thirteen semi-permanently coupled oil tanks cars. Runs from Dolores to Wunpost. Usually through Gemco in the dark, but can run at any time. Recently increased service from about three times a week to closer to four times a week.)

Los Nietos and Valla (Santa Fe Springs)

(Los Nietos – Los Nietos Road, Santa Fe Springs, CA – limited views from Los Nietos and from Smith.)

(Valla – 9193 Santa Fe Springs Road, Santa Fe Springs – no view possible, no access, can barely tell there is a yard there.)

LOA33R Los Nietos Switcher   Mon-Fri
(On duty 0600. Captive switcher – serves industries on the industrial spurs to the east of Los Nietos Yard, west of Norwalk, including pipe, chemical, and plastics places. Usually done for the day by 1200, but if busy, can work deep into the afternoon.)

LOA35R	Patata Local	Mon-Fri

(On duty 0800. Heads south from Los Nietos through Downey to South Gate on Los Nietos Sub and Patata Industrial Lead. Works South Gate, Central Metal in Firestone Park off the San Pedro Sub. On return, runs north through Los Nietos Yard and then backs in. Can be as early as 1330 or as last as 1700.)

LOA36R	Valla Local	Mon-Fri

(On duty 0630 at Valla Yard. MWF they serve customers in Valla Yard, Los Nietos, Santa Fe Springs, Pico Rivera and Los Angeles, and along the La Habra Sub. TuTh they switch Pacific Plastics in Brea on the Brea Industrial Lead and can work Santa Fe Springs if needed. Sometime switches up and goes to Brea on Friday instead of Thursday. Has the ability to run to Basta if there is work, but presently not servicing Cargill, so not going that far. Power ties up on east end of Valla about 1600.)

Buena Park

(Buena Park – 6498 Regio Avenue, Buena Park, CA – can view power from street.)

LOA38R	Norwalk Local	Sun-Thu

(On duty 2000 M-Th, 1300 on Sun. Serves customers in Norwalk, Downey, Carmenita, and LA on the Santa Ana Industrial Lead and Los Nietos Sub. Heads out of Regio to the La Mirada storage tracks to get their loads for the night. Spot cars for the cement plant. Shove across Shoemaker and spot cars for Weyerhaeuser. Works Coca-Cola in Downey)

LOA39R	Buena Park Local	Mon-Fri

(On duty 0600. Serves customers along the Santa Ana Industrial Lead in Buena Park, La Mirada, and Cerritos, getting back to County Line about 0900 or 1000. Switches the La Mirada Storage tracks there for a while and then shoves loads into the SP industrial park, working those industries and parking at Regio when done.)

Anaheim Wye/West Anaheim (Anaheim)

(Anaheim Wye – 1599 W. Mable Street, Anaheim, CA – very easy to photograph from street.)

LOA31R	Marlboro Local	Mon-Fri

(On duty 1331. Works Anaheim and Orange. Street runs on Santa Ana between 1400 and 1700. 1430 is a good bet for the Lemon St wigwag. Crosses the SCAX Orange Sub to get to Ganahl Lumber, Hobbs Trucking, and Diversified CPC International. Goes further east when needed to Fisher Printing, fix, and Christian in Orange.)

LOA32	Costa Mesa Local	Mon-Thu

(On duty 0600. On MW, serves the Costa Mesa/Santa Ana area. Street runs between 0645-0730 & 1000-1100. Takes the SCAX Orange Sub to Santa Ana and then regains the Santa Ana Industrial Lead. Back to Anaheim between 1000 and 1200. On TuTh runs down the Stanton Industrial Lead working the industries all along on its way back. Although only running four days a week, this job has a huge list of customers. Back in Anaheim 1100)

LOA44	COFI Turn (calls self "Anaheim" on radio)	Mon-Fri

(On duty 0700. Hauls from Anaheim, Buena Park, and Los Nietos to City of Industry and West Colton. Uses power LOQ25 left on the wye. Builds its train from cars left along the Santa Ana Industrial Lead by the locals. Can take hours to be ready to go. Often see from I-5 in Anaheim building its train from 0730 to 0900. In City of Industry about 1000. Runs through Pomona between 1050 and 1150. Hits West Colton as early as 1150. Can have an extra run on Saturdays if needed.)

City of Industry

(COFI Yard – South Azusa Avenue, City of Industry, CA – some okay views from the Azusa overpass.)

ACICI	Auto Hauler	Sat-Mon

(On duty 1003. Runs autoracks from City of Industry to West Colton, to Mira Loma, and back to City of Industry. Call time questionable, as has also been spotted about 1800. Likely that this train is simply an extra.)

ICICIR	Baretables	As needed
ICIELR		
ICILAR		
ICILBR		
ICIWLR		

(On duty when needed. Baretable moves in and out of City of Industry keep the yard moving. Baretables are hauled to and picked up from North Walnut, El Segundo, ICTF, Montclair, and Los Angeles. Symbol is IxxxxR – with reverse moves appropriately symboled.)

LOS27	San Gabriel Switcher	Mon-Fri

(On duty 0605. Services customers on the Basset Metrolink Sub from El Monte, Temple City, to Baldwin Park. Will hear DS refer to as either the 27 or the San Gabriel Switcher. Customers include Performance Sheets, Accu Chem, Mercado Latino, Custom Alloy, Coastal Wood, Flinte, Lind, Nichols Lumber, Cascade Steel, and Reliable Wholesale in Temple City.)

LOS29	Industrial Switcher	Mon-Fri

(On duty 1515. Alhambra Sub switcher. Serves industries around the yard. Has been spotted working the wye at Valley Blvd near La Puente. Power is often mid-train. Works alongside Valley Blvd in Avocado Heights. Customers include CF Foods, Girrard, La Corr, Engines and Sealed Air.)

LOS41	759AM COFI	Mon-Fri

(On duty 0600. Los Angeles Sub road switcher. Works exclusively within COFI, including the Towers Industrial Park along Don Julian Road in City of Industry between the two UP Subs. Has a long customer list. Power is often mid-train. Finishes about 1100.)

LOS42	7PM COFI	Sun-Thu

(On duty 2000. Los Angeles Sub road switcher. Shoves into Azusa Yard to build train. Goes east to Walnut. Customers include Tropicana, GE Refrigerator, GE Stoves, GE Washers, Hoover, and Pro Pak. Once train is built shoves to MP26 and pulls back to Lemon Ave. to enter the Customer Zone. Once the work is completed at Lemon Ave– for GE and Tropicana, shoves back to the Main pull down and serves Hoover, and ProPak.)

LOS49	Baldwin Park Local	Mon-Fri

(On duty 1730. Serves Azusa Industrial Lead and part of the Metrolink San Gabriel Sub. Serves Reichold, Veolia, Criterion, Bolcof, Davis Wire, and Pacific Panel on the San Gabriel Sub. Can work as far as Azusa, heading north above the 210 Freeway and serving Miller and others, but only when needed and generally on Wed or Fri only. Finishes about 0100.)

MCIWC	COFI Hauler (eastbound)	Tue, Wed, Thu, Sat

(On duty 1200. Departs about 1400. Carries City of Industry and Chino outbound manifest loads to West Colton. Arrives about 2100. Has been spotted on a Friday too.)

YCI19	COFI Yard Switcher	Mon-Fri

(On duty 0730. Works the ramp, picking up cars off the north and south drills.)

YCI20	COFI Yard Switcher	Daily

(On duty 0405. Works the ramp, picking up cars off the north and south drills.)

YCI26	COFI Yard Switcher	Daily

(On duty 1500. Works the ramp, picking up cars off the north and south drills.)

YCI30	COFI Yard Switcher	Daily

(On duty 2101. Works the ramp, picking up cars off the north and south drills.)

Chino

(Chino – 13932 Monte Vista Avenue, Chino, CA – not accessible can't be photographed.)

LOB28	Chino Industry Switcher	Mon-Fri

(On duty at 0700. Switches the rabbit warren of industrial spurs and tracks within the China Industrial Park, never coming out to the main.)

| LOB29 | Chino Local | Mon-Fri |

(On duty 0700. Runs Chino to Pomona, working industries on the lead along the way, making it almost to the LA and Alhambra Subs, but not quite. They also switch the spur to the west. Are back by 1500.)

| LOS48 | Chino Local | Sun-Thu |

(On duty 2030. Starts in Montclair and vans to Chino. Train heads from Chino to City of Industry with cars from LOB28 and LOB29. Drops off empties at COFI. Switches Azusa yard and then heads to the north side of COFI off the ISO, west of Turnbull Canyon Road. Picks up loads which it hauls back to Chino.)

Mira Loma (Jurupa Valley)

(Mira Loma – Mission Boulevard, Jurupa Valley, CA – can be viewed and photographed from street.)

(Mira Loma Auto Facility – Etiwanda Avenue and Harrel Street, Jurupa Valley, CA – not accessible, but on far east end, can occasionally see locomotives from street.)

(Arlington Yard – 5809 Jurupa Avenue, Riverside, CA – not accessible, can kind of view from back of commercial buildings there.)

(TXI Riverside Cement - Rubidoux Boulevard between El Revino and Agua Mansa, in Riverside – not accessible or viewable.)

| AMLDOR | Autoracks | Daily |

(On duty 2030. Cycles empty autoracks from Mira Loma to Long Beach to be delivered to the car importers in the Harbor. Seems to run pretty randomly, despite having a scheduled on duty time Recent departure times have been 0300, 1330, and 2100. Takes between five to ten hours to get to Long Beach.)

| LOB32 | Montclair Switcher | Mon-Fri |

(On duty 0830. Works the LA Sub west to Pomona, dropping off loaded westbounds and picking up empty eastbounds. Often at Ventura Foods in Ontario between 1230 and 1330. Also works Montclair Yard if needed. Switches Potlatch Siding along Mt. Vernon Ave before heading back. Seen in Pomona as late as 1500 westbound and 1700 eastbound. Uses road power, looks like a hauler.)

| LOB33 | Crestmore Local | Sun-Thu |

(On duty 0600 at TXI Riverside Cement in Crestmore. Heads west with empties to Mira Loma, where it builds a train of loads at about 0900. Back on the branch between 1100 and 0100. Calls DS 30 to occupy the number one main between Mira Loma and the Pedley Wye, which means they are eastbound. Can go to Champion Lumber on BNSF in Highgrove if needed. Power ties down at Riverside Cement out of public view.)

LOB34R	PM Mira Loma Switcher	Mon-Fri

(On duty 0500. Switches the cars from the inbound LOQ47 , blocking all cars for the locals LOB33/lOB35R/LOB40. Also will pull the empty's from Coca Cola , and spot and pull the industries at the Space Center just north of the yard and at the San Sevaine Industrial Park. All customers are in Mira Loma.)

LOB35	AM Mira Loma Switcher ("Cheeseburger Local")	Saturday only

(On duty 0930. Heads east down the LA Sub and enters the BNSF San Bernardino Sub in Riverside in order to reach and work Reliable Lumber and Champion Lumber in Highgrove. Runs back to Mira Loma where it serves a limited number of the LOB35R customers on the Dixon Branch including Coke and Temple Inland.

LOB35R	AM Mira Loma Switcher	Tue-Fri

(On duty 0930. Leaves the yard by about 1200. Works the Dixon Branch which heads north out of Mira Loma clockwise around Ontario, and ends back in Mira Loma just past the Nestle warehouse at Grapevine & De Forest Circle. This includes Coca Cola, GAF, Liqui Box, Levecke, Weyerhaeuser, and Vanport among others including the San Sevaine Industrial area. Also works the Baxter Lead west of the yard by Philadelphia, which may just be used for storage now.)

LOB38R	Arlington Local	Tue, Wed, Thu

(On duty 0530 TuWe and 0849 on Thu. Starts at Arlington Yard, using LOB40 power. Works the yard as needed. Runs down the Rohr Spur on Thu, and sometimes Tue, serving customers on the twisting run alongside Riverside Airport. Otherwise, switches Crest Steel.)

LOB40	CalPro Hauler	Mon-Fri

(On duty 1900. Crew vans over to Arlington Yard. Takes the empty train from Arlington back to Mira Loma to set out empties for the LOB45. Then switches out the International Paper cars. Switches out all Arlington cars and Crest Steel cars. After leaving Mira Loma and arriving at MP51 spot and pull Crest Steel. Head back to Arlington. Believe this job also delivers bad order cars to CalPro/TTX. In ML.)

LOB45	Mira Loma Hauler	Mon, Wed, Fri

(On duty 1930 at Colton. Vans to Mira Loma. Uses the power left by LOQ47. Gathers all cars for Colton and builds outbound train. Waits for LOB40 to bring in pickup pulls for the night. Runs around train and then pulls it into Colton.)

SMLML	Special Switcher	As needed

(On duty when needed. Extra jobs use this symbol.)

YML01	AM Auto Facility Switcher	Daily

(On duty 0600. Not actually switched by UP, but rather a private contractor. Use UP Green Goats to shove inbound loaded autoracks into the facility and then switches them so that Inter-Rail Group can transload them. On average, 17 to 25 railcars an hour are unloaded. When the autoracks are empty, Progress Rail inspects them and makes needed repairs. The cars are then built into outbound trains. Possible to photograph when locomotives are on the tail track at east end. First job finishes up at 1330.)

YML02	PM Auto Facility Switcher	Daily

(On duty 1400. See YML01 for details. Second job finishes up at 2200.)

YML03	Night Auto Facility Switcher	Daily

(On duty 2200. See YML01 for details. Third job finishes up at 0600.)

Kaiser (Fontana)

(Kaiser – Loop Road, Fontana, CA – no possible way to access, but can see from freeway.)

LOH32	Ontario Local (railfan nickname "The Sunkist")	Mon-Fri

(On duty 0600. Normally uses two gensets. Yards the inbound LOQ32 at Kaiser, and then builds a "city work" train at Kaiser Yard before proceeding west to the Coast Grain facility just west of the yard – the old Vina Vista. MWF and as needed, crew continues to North Ontario to service two customers on the Sunkist Lead: Grove Lumber and Partners Alliance, who occasionally gets reefers for loading. Normally arrives at North Ontario between 1100 and 1300 but varies due to actual arrival at Kaiser of the LOQ32 train. Upon completion of work returns to Kaiser Yard with pull cars.)

LOH42	Guasti Local	Sun-Thu

(On duty 1000. Normally uses three gensets. Crew builds their "city work" train at Kaiser Yard then proceeds west to service customers on the Johnson Wax and K-Mart leads. Then takes loads to Biagi Brothers the beer distributor at Guasti. The Guasti move usually occurs after 1400. Upon completion of work returns to Kaiser Yard with pull cars.)

LOH43	Declezville Local	Mon-Fri

(On duty 1400. Normally uses two gensets. Crew builds their "city work" train at Kaiser Yard and then proceeds east to Declezville in South Fontana to service customers there. On TuTh this job also services the industries on the south side of the main track at Kaiser Yard. Customers include plastics plants, pipe manufacturers, and grain.)

LOH45	California Steel & Hauler Job (calls self "Kaiser" on radio)	Mon-Fri

(On duty 1830. Normally has road power. Crew builds their "city work" train at Kaiser Yard then proceeds up the Kaiser Lead to industries at the old Kaiser Steel plant including California Steel Industries. Upon completion of customer work and return to Kaiser Yard this job builds the outbound train and hauls it to the West Colton receiving yard, usually about 0100. After yarding their train, the power is taken to the departure yard to be available for the LOQ32 in the morning.)

West Colton (Bloomington)

(West Colton – South Willow Avenue and West Slover Avenue, Rialto, CA – can be viewed from Sierra, Cedar, Riverside, and the most famous, Pepper, which is the only one with a place to park.)

(Old Colton – 9th and K Streets, Colton, CA – if power is there, fairly easy to see and shoot.)

(Cabazon – Johnson Lane along the 10, Cabazon, CA – can view from street, but not a great photo.)

LOQ25	Anaheim Hauler	Mon-Fri

(On duty 2130. Leaves WC about 2230. Takes the balloon track at Pepper Street, running through City of Industry as it hauls manifest freight from West Colton to Los Nietos and West Anaheim. Arrives in Anaheim about 0230 and leaves power on Broadway Wye for the next day's LOA44.)

LOQ32	Kaiser Hauler	Mon-Fri
LOQ32S		

(On duty 0600. Crew comes on duty at Kaiser and vans to West Colton. Train departs east, around the balloon track at Pepper Street, proceeds west to Kaiser Yard. Scheduled West Colton departure is 0900. Usually will use the last LOH45's power. An extra hauler is called on Sundays using train symbol LOQ32S.)

LOQ35	Gemco Hauler	Wed-Mon

(On duty 2000. Can leave between 2130 and 2200, but sometimes waits for congestion at West Colton to clear. Takes the balloon track at Pepper Street. Moves manifest freight from West Colton to Weeds/East Yard and Gemco in Van Nuys. Carries cars for Oxnard and Guadalupe. Arrives at Gemco between 0230 and 0530.)

LOQ47	Mira Loma Hauler	Sun, Tue, Thu

(On duty 2100. Moves manifest freight from West Colton to Mira Loma. Takes the balloon track at Pepper Street to head west on Alhambra Sub, making a drop at Montclair. Then reverses direction in Pomona, heading east on the LA Sub. Can stop to do work at Montclair Yard if needed. Arrives in Mira Loma between 0200 and 0430. Leaves power for the next LOB45 in Mira Loma.)

LOQ91	Mojave Flyer	Sun-Wed-Fri

(On duty approx 0200. Moves manifest freight from West Colton to Mojave. Leaves West Colton before dawn. Heads up the Mojave Sub, over Cajon Pass, arriving at Mojave between 0800 and 1000.)

M-WCLBAR1	WinckleBar (BNSF Train)	Mon-Sat
MWC7BJ		

(On duty 1900. Leaves around 1945 or so. BNSF power – BNSF transfer to Barstow. Mostly made up of empties. Cars include grain hoppers, ADM corn syrup tank cars, hazmat tanks, boxcars, and occasional skyboxes. Cycles bad-orders for repair. Uses power left at West Colton by last M-BARWCL1)

MWCCI	Tropicana Shuttle	Mon-Thu, Sat

(On duty 0700. Runs around the balloon track at West Colton about 0845 to 0945, heading west to set out manifest cars for City of Industry, City of Industry UP, and Chino. It also picks up the Tropicana empties for LATC. Heads further west to LATC, where it picks up loaded Tropicana's to take back to COFI. Arrives LATC about 1400, departs eastbound about 1600.)

MWCEC	El Centro Hauler	Sun, Tue, Thu, Sat

(On duty 1500. Heads east at Pepper. Moves manifest freight from West Colton to Indio and El Centro. Sets out cars, and sometimes a road unit at Indio for switching or to replace the helper. At Indio they serve AC Houston Lumber, an LPG facility, and a covered hopper transload facility. At El Centro they leave cars for local jobs and Ferromex interchange.)

MWCFR	Fresno Hauler	Mon, Wed, Fri

(On duty 1000. Heads north at Pepper, up the Palmdale Cutoff. Moves manifest freight to Bakersfield and Fresno over the Mojave Sub. Carries a lot of reefers. The reverse, MFRWC, arrives West Colton about 1300 on SuWF.)

MWCJY	J-Yard Hauler aka Colton Crawler	Sun, Tue, Thu

(On duty 2300. Really a turn, not a hauler. Heads out the balloon track at Pepper to go west. Moves manifest freight, including Chevron loads, from West Colton to 4th Street Yard and J-Yard. Then returns to West Colton with traffic from J-Yard and 4th Street.)

MWCLB	Long Beach Hauler	Tue-Sun

(On duty 2130. Heads around the balloon track at Pepper to go west. Hauls from West Colton to Long Beach. Makes a set out at the east end of Mead Yard. Makes a set out of PHL cars on the AB lead between Crucero and Gaspur for one of the PHL jobs to pick up. Carries PHL, ECXX dirty dirt, scrap gondolas, and empty wells. Arrives Mead about 0030.)

MWCWC	Colton Yard Transfer	As needed

(On duty when needed. Ad hoc symbol for extra switcher and/or hauler jobs.)

RWCWCG	Robertson's Ready Mix Rock Train	Mon-Fri +
RWCWCC		

(On duty time varies. Cabazon to Rosewood train carries rocks to the conveyer south of Conoco. Has a GEVO on either end. Runs as a shuttle turn. There is a crew change at Ice Deck. Some recent times: westbound at Ontario 1530, at East Redondo 1500 at Colton Xing 1259, and Pomona 1553 – eastbound 2042 into Ice Deck Siding and 2058 at Pomona. Not clear when it changes from C code to G code. Works weekends if needed.)

YWC20R	Hump Job	Tue-Sun

(On duty 0630 Works with at least one FRA-exempted-for-hump-use-only SD38-2. Picks up cars from arrival yard at CP Sierra and shoves them to Crest where they hump the train.)

YWC21R	Hump Job	Tue-Sun

(On duty 0745. Works with at least one FRA-exempted-for-hump-use-only SD38-2. Picks up cars from arrival yard at CP Sierra and shoves them to Crest where they hump the train.)

YWC25R	730 Trim Job	Tue-Sat

(On duty 0700. Pulls trains eastward out of the bowl to the departure tracks. Seen working midday at Pepper. Generally has SD40-2s. Works until about 1430.)

| YWC28 | 730 Trim Job | Tue-Sun |

(On duty 0700. Pulls trains eastward out of the bowl to the departure tracks. Seen working midday at Pepper. Generally has SD40-2s. Finishes up about 1530.)

| YWC30R | Early PM Hump | Daily |

(On duty 1430. Works with at least one FRA-exempted-for-hump-use-only SD38-2. Picks up cars from arrival yard at CP Sierra and shoves them to Crest where they hump the train.)

| YWC31R | Late PM Hump | Daily |

(On duty 1545. Works with at least one FRA-exempted-for-hump-use-only SD38-2. Picks up cars from arrival yard at CP Sierra and shoves them to Crest where they hump the train.)

| YWC34R | 1530 Trim Job | Tue-Sun |

(On duty 1500. Pulls trains eastward out of the bowl to the departure tracks. Generally has SD40-2s. Works until about 2300.)

| YWC35R | Trim Job | Unknown |

(On duty 1530. Pulls trains eastward out of the bowl to the departure tracks. Generally has SD40-2s. Works until about 2330.)

| YWC36 | Trim Job | Unknown |

(On duty 1559. Pulls trains eastward out of the bowl to the departure tracks. Generally has SD40-2s. Finishes anywhere from 1700 to 0000.)

| YWC40R | Hump Job | Daily |

(On duty 2230. Works with at least one FRA-exempted-for-hump-use-only SD38-2. Picks up cars from arrival yard at CP Sierra and shoves them to Crest where they hump the train.)

| YWC42R | Hump Job | Unknown |

(On duty 2345. Works with at least one FRA-exempted-for-hump-use-only SD38-2. Picks up cars from arrival yard at CP Sierra and shoves them to Crest where they hump the train. Finishes in the AM.)

| YWC43R | Trim Job | Unknown |

(On duty 2300. Pulls trains eastward out of the bowl to the departure tracks. Generally has SD40-2s. Works until about 0630.)

| YWC44 | Trim Job | Unknown |

(On duty 0000. Pulls trains eastward out of the bowl to the departure tracks. Generally has SD40-2s. Finishes around 0800.)

| YWC45R | 2230 Trim Job | Daily |

(On duty 2230. Pulls trains eastward out of the bowl to the departure tracks. Generally has SD40-2s. Works until about 0630.)

YWC50R	Trim Job	Unknown

(On duty 1630. Pulls trains eastward out of the bowl to the departure tracks. Generally has SD40-2s. A trim job on duty this time has been seen serving the GATX plant at Pepper at about 2200. Might be this job. Finishes up around 0130.)

YWC54	Lowe's Local/Rialto Local	Mon-Fri

(On duty 1600. On Mon and Thu heads to Beaumont with road power to the Lowe's Flatbed Distribution Facility. Has centerbeams, boxcars, and covered hoppers. Returns to West Colton on Tue and Fri. On Wed it runs with yard power, up the Mojave Sub to Bench, and then down the Rialto Sub, to Orange County Lumber, the last customer on the Rialto Sub. Normally brings in 2-5 cars consisting of a mix of centerbeams and lumber boxcars. Back to WC about 2100. Drops train at CP Sierra.)

YWC66	Roustabout	Wed and Sat only

(On duty 1030. works as conventional job with an engineer on Wed and Sat to spot and pull CalPortland Cement at Slover Mountain. This job is reported to deliver and pick up cars at the GATX facility at Pepper. Finishes around 1300 to 1400.)

YWC66R	Trim Job	Sun-Tue, Thu, Fri

(On duty 1030. Pulls trains eastward out of the bowl to the departure tracks. Generally has SD40-2s.)

YWC80	Old Colton Local	Daily

(On duty 0000. Called at Colton although picks up power at West Colton and then runs train to Old Colton. Among its customers is Pacific Rail Industries, who receive aggregates for transloading in an area of Old Colton Yard. Takes power back to the 500 pocket near Riverside Avenue in front of the Trim Tower for YWC86. Seems to finish up around 0400.)

YWC86	Riverside Local	Mon-Fri

(On duty 0900. On MWF it switches ConAgra at Ice Deck. On TuTh and sometimes Wed shoves down the Riverside Industrial Lead, street running about 1000 past the 9th Street wigwag. Heads to Cascade Lumber in the old Griffin Wheel complex, and Lehigh Cement and Sigma Stretch Film on either side of Atlanta Avenue by the Moreno Valley Freeway. Finishes between 1300 and 1600. Drops train at CP Sierra. Leaves power at Riverside Avenue for YWC80.)

Additional manifests out of West Colton

MWCFW- Fort Worth
MWCNP – North Platte
MWCPXX – Phoenix (Only runs as an extra now)
MWCRO – Salt Lake City (Roper Yard)
MWCRV – Roseville
MWCRVB- Roseville
QWCEW - Houston
QWCTU - Tucson

Littlerock (Palmdale)

(Little Rock – 7316 East Avenue T, Palmdale, CA – does not appear to be accessible.)

RVUVU   Vulcan Rock Train.   Daily
            (On duty about 2000 Mon-Sat, and 1000 Sun. Leaves Little Rock on the Mojave Sub after
            the Metrolink. Passes Newhall at 2230 on its way to the old Conrock facility in Sun
            Valley. Leaves CP Vulcan at 0400 on return trip, hitting Little Rock about 0630. On
            Sunday, departs CP Vulcan about 1700, hitting Little Rock about 1900.)

Oxnard

(Oxnard – 299 East 5th Street, Oxnard, CA – can see from street, but power is often parked behind
freight cars.)

LOF63   Oxnard Local   Mon-Fri
            (On duty 0600, usually done working by 1200. Serves all customers between Somis and
            Ventura as well as Santa Paula Branch, which is currently out of service just east of
            Saticoy due to bridge failure. Only current regular shipper, International Paper, has shut
            down Santa Paula plant and three other shippers have not had service in some time, so
            future Branch operation is uncertain. Current regular traffic is Hagle Lumber on Hagle
            Spur in Somis, International Paper on Weyerhaeuser Spur in Camarillo, Proctor &
            Gamble, M&I, Diversified Building Materials, Terminal Freezer in Oxnard, and Stock
            Lumber and Ventura Coastal in Ventura. Also pulls east traffic on Tues. and Fri. from VCY
            to stage at Oxnard Yard for LOF66 Guadalupe Turn to pick up along with Oxnard Local
            pulls.)

Guadalupe and San Luis Obispo

(Guadalupe, 299 East 5th Street, Oxnard, CA – can see from street, but power is often parked behind
freight cars.)

(San Luis Obispo, 1011 Railroad Avenue, San Luis Obispo – nice open PM shot of the helpers.)

(Wunpost, Route 101, Wunpost, CA – can see in the distance but cannot access and no good photo.)

HSQSQ   San Luis Obispo Helpers   As needed
            (On duty when needed. Union Pacific keeps helpers at the San Luis Obispo station to
            assist trains over Cuesta. They are only called when needed, often times for the
            OWPDO.)

| LOF66 | Guadalupe Turn | Tue, Fri |

(On duty at 1401. If train is already built by LOL30, can be brought on duty up to - but not over - two hours early. This is the return leg for this Gemco crew. Handles all short work between, but not including, Surf and Ventura. Active shippers include a lumber distributer at Elwood and Vandenburg AFB (Narlon. LOF66 picks up east traffic at Oxnard. No longer does ANY short work east of Ventura other than Oxnard pick-up. Power comes from last LOF67.)

| LOL30 | Guadalupe Local | Mon-Fri |

(On duty 0800. Builds the LOF66. Builds its own train at Guadalupe. Heads north on MWF. Can go all the way to SLO if needed. On TuTh, runs south to Surf, and then up the Lompoc Industrial Lead to Lompoc, where it gets in some street running. Reverses direction and shoves up the White Hills Industrial Lead with a caboose that is left in Lompoc Yard. Can run north to Calendar after Lompoc if needed.)

| OWPDO | Oil Cans | sked for Tuesday but run about every other day |

(On duty when called, often around 1700 to 1800. Leaves Wunpost when train is full – can be any time day or night, but more likely near 0000. UP gets the call and sends an extra crew to Wunpost to bring it to San Luis Obispo where there is a crew change to an SLO to LA crew, who take it to Main St. in Los Angeles where a Basin crew takes over for the run to Dolores and spotting it. Has 6 cuts of 13 cars for a total of 78 cars.)

Mojave

(Mojave – 15138 Sierra Highway, Mojave, CA – can see from street, but not a great shot.)

| LOP51 | Blitz Local | Daily |

(On duty 0800. Heads over to the Chaffee siding north of the yard and brings back the LOP 83 if left there. Runs up to CalPortland Cement in Creal on the Oak Creek Industrial Lead. Returns to Mojave to classify pulls. Then build outbound trains RMJSTC, RMJLVC, which are CPC units trains to Stockton and Vegas, and also builds the LOP92.)

| LOP53 | Monolith Local | Mon-Fri |

(On duty 1400. Works the tank farm up the Lone Pine Sub. Goes to Monolith on MWF to work the cement plant east of Tehachapi. Heads south on TuThSa to Antelope Valley with tank cars for the old Great Lakes Carbon Lead as well as the tank car farm just south of Mojave. Serves Progress Rail and Niklor Chemical. Sometimes their work will be done by an MMJMJ, especially the Monolith runs.)

| LOP82 | Lone Pine Local | Mon-Sat |

(On duty 1600. Runs up the Lone Pine Sub to Searles to interchange with the Trona. Most of the time returns to Mojave about midnight. Can run in the morning on Saturday and Sunday if needed. Crew can be used on OTNLB if needed.)

LOP92	Mojave Flyer	Tue-Thu-Sat

(On duty 0300. Mojave to West Colton hauler. Originates in Mojave and runs with whatever cars are needed to West Colton. Can be built by an MMJMJ and then be left at Ansel or Fleta for a road crew.)

MMJMJ	Mojave Yard Transfer	As needed (most days)

(On duty when needed. Builds long trains so the road crew will not have to do all the doubling over and air testing for the Flyer LOP92 and takes the train out to Ansel or Fleta. Can also break up inbound LOQ91. Two MMJMJs can work at the same time if traffic warrants.)

OTNLB	Trona Train	4 to 5 times a week

(On duty when needed. Hauls loaded potash from the Trona to the aggregate transload facility in Long Beach owned by Metro Ports. Goes down the Mojave Sub to West Colton. Runs to PHL's Pier G Yard.)

El Centro

(El Centro – 364 West Main Street, El Centro, CA – can view and photograph from street.)

LOE34	Calexico Local	Mon-Fri

(On duty 0100. Runs southeast toward the border town of Calexico to interchange with the Ferromex local. Arrives Calexico 0200. Crew ties down the train and vans into Mexico. The van waits for the FXE crew coming up from the Mexicali Yard. Change crews at the border, in view of Customs. The UP crew will then slowly drag the train into the US while being inspected by Customs. Once their rear end clears the border they accelerate to 10 mph into the Calexico Yard, parking next to their own waiting southbound train. Then they take the southbound train to the border and change crews with the waiting FXE crew. The train typically remains stationary for the southbound customs inspection to keep from blocking the many main streets in downtown Mexicali. The FXE crew departs for the Mexicali Yard just before dusk. Meanwhile, the UP crew vans back to the northbound train for the El Centro run. There is a rail curfew in Mexicali preventing the FXE crew from departing later than 0630. If the southbound UP Train gets delayed, the interchange waits for the next day.)

LOE35	El Centro Yard Switcher	Sun-Thu

(On duty 2000. Classifies the MWCEC, building the next day's LOE34, LOE36, and LOE27. Then builds a MECWC, leaving the units on the west end. Air tests the hauler before heading off to Simplot to pull empties.)

LOE36	Plaster City Job	Sun-Fri

(On duty 0700. On TuTh runs west to Plaster City first to work US Gypsum, bringing cars to the Southern California Railroad. Also works Accu Chem, Westway, Cemex, and Temple Inland, Can deliver cars to Carrizo Gorge when they are running.)

LOE37   Calipatria Local   Mon-Sat
               (On duty 0400. Runs northeast to Spreckles Sugar in Brawly. Has about eight additional
               customers on the Imperial Sub.)

MECWC   El Centro Hauler (westbound)   Sun, Mon, Wed, Fri
               (On duty late afternoon, Departs for West Colton around dinner time. Makes a pickup in
               Indio. Arrives at West Colton around 2200.)

Amtrak

8ᵗʰ Street Yard (Los Angeles)

(8th Street Yard – 2503 East Olympic Boulevard, Los Angeles, CA. Can view from Olympic. Switching jobs can use road power that pulled train in or switcher.)

YL220   Unknown
> (On duty 0630 – 1430. Generally performs last minute switching of train 14, deadheads it to LAUPT, and then deadheads either #3 or #1 back to 8th street yard for servicing and switching. Switches #3 or #1 as necessary during the day.)

YL230   Unknown
> (On duty 0600 – 1400. Does any last minute switching, brings 761 or 1761 to the depot, then either vans or brings #3 or #1 back to 8th street yard. Brings 566 to the depot and vans back, or brings #3 or #1 then switches that train out.)

YL240   Unknown
> (On duty 1459 – 2259. Generally completes switching the SW Chief, brings it to the platform, then retrieves 583 and 798 and brings them back to the yard for any switching and servicing.)

YL250   Unknown
> (On duty 1700 – 0100. Does any miscellaneous work around the yard and then vans to LAUPT to bring 589 and 595 to 8th street. Performs switching on the Surfliners as necessary.)

YL260   Unknown
> (On duty 2201 to 0601. Vans out to LAUPT and recovers train 11, brings it to the yard and performs any switching of all overnight trains. Brings 562 and 564 to the depot as a double set in the morning before vanning back to 8th street to finish out their night.)

RYL270   Unknown
> (Relief job which works various shifts on different days.)

RYL280   Unknown
> (Relief job which works various shifts on different days.)

Coast Rail Services

Adams Steel/Coast Rail   Mon-Fri

(Anaheim – 3250 East Frontera Street, Anaheim, CA – not accessible.)

(BN GP9s and a Topeka Cab GP7u are used to switch a hopper logistics distribution center hidden in the back of Adams Steel Monday to Friday. Finishes up about 1600. Also does random scrapping of locomotives when they get the work. Have one Topeka Cab GP7u in Coat Rail colors and two GP9s still in BN colors. There is a third ex BN GP9 that they are using as a parts donor. The west side of facility can be viewed from the top floor of the Embassy Suites Hotel on Frontera.)

BNSF Logistics Center/Coast Rail   Suspended

(Fontana – Kaiser Way, Fontana, CA – not accessible but can see a little from the street.)

(BNSF Logistics Center was previously switched by Coast Rail with a GP9 & SW10. They still have two units parked there. Gate is sometimes open on weekdays and Saturdays, but units are parked beyond the internal guard shack.)

Ferromex

(For all intents and purposes, Mexicali is beyond the scope of this book, and the Ferromex information is utterly incomplete. I provide it here as this much is known to me and someone railfanning around El Centro is likely to hit Mexicali too.)

Mexicali

Ferromex/UP Interchange Job   Mon-Fri
On duty 0400. Has to be at the US border at 0430 to meet the UP job.)

Ferromex Local Job   Daily
(Heads south of the yard around 1300. Performs industrial work along the mainline. Works Agrovizion Integradora S.A de C.V. & Stone Container, which causes it to need to back across Highway 2.)

Ferromex Yard Job   Unknown
(Works in the afternoons.)

Ferromex Intermodal   Unknown
(Arrives from the south between 1500 and 1700.)

Los Angeles Junction

A Yard (Vernon) (BNSF Subsidiary, uses BNSF four-axle power)

(LAJ A – Yard – 4433 Exchange Avenue, Vernon, CA, not accessible but can kind of see from street.)

(LAJ B – Yard – 4757 District Boulevard, Vernon, CA, not accessible but if working, can get an idea what they are doing from the street.)

(LAJ C – Yard – 5710 Bandini Boulevard, Vernon, CA, mostly inaccessible, but if power is parked at front gate, a good shot from a public place. Can be empty at times.)

(Bell Yard – G Street between 1st and Long Beach Freeway, utterly inaccessible, but you can see from afar with binoculars or a telephoto if you are checking on the M-LACBAR consist for some reason.)

Y-VRN1171	117 Tramp Job	Mon-Fri
	(On duty 0600. Begins by putting together its train in A Yard and then heads northwest over the river with its deliveries for the day.)	
Y-VRN1181	Strategic Materials Job	Unknown
	(On duty time unknown. This job is dedicated to switching a recycling plant, Strategic Materials Inc. The crew is directed by plant personnel.)	
Y-VRN1191	119 Tramp Job	Mon-Fri
	(On duty 0759. Begins by switching A and B Yards. If needed, then works the industrial sidings near the yard.)	
Y-VRN2271	227 Job	Mon-Fri
	(On duty 1400. Puts together an M-LACBAR for the BNSF, including putting BNSF power on it. Shoves the M-LACBAR east to Bell Yard, leaving it behind the National Guard Armory there, where it is inaccessible. Also switches A Yard as needed.)	
Y-VRN2281	228 Job	Mon-Fri
	(On duty 1559. Works local industries in the Central Manufacturing District, CMD. At 1730 it crosses Atlantic at the LA River. A few minutes later it crosses Slauson at the LA River. Then crosses Eastern at Slauson, heading to the Long Laguna/C Yard area.)	
Y-VRN3351	335 Job	Unknown
	(On duty 2230. Switches the Long Laguna/C yard area and industries south of C Yard)	

Pacific Harbor Line (part of Anacostia & Pacific)

Wilmington CA

(Pier A Yard – 510 South Fries Avenue, Wilmington, CA – can view from street, but chain link fence blocks much.)

(Pier B Yard – 1544 Pier B Street, Long Beach, CA – can view and photograph from street.)

Pier A and Main Line Jobs

7AM Pier A Yard Switcher   Daily
> (On duty 0700. Mostly switches Pier A Yard, but also works the San Pedro Sub along the West Basin if needed, including the Gaffey Street Sub. Can run to auto yards or back down Fries to Pasha to switch the Borax hoppers. Has also been the 6AM Pier A Yard Switcher.)

5PM West Basin Job   Daily
> (On duty 1700. Works industries along West Basin in San Pedro. Leaves Pier A with as much as 3,000 tons. Often has to shove up to 2,000 tons of that into ConocoPhillips. ConocoPhillips is on the Tosco Lead, which goes under the 110 Freeway. Shoves up the Gaffey Street Sub to Rancho LPG – but maybe only in the winter. Brings mixed freight back to pier A backing around the wye into the yard)

Auto Switcher   Mon-Fri
> (On duty 1000 to 1100. Work the auto importer yards – most recently with the Progress Rail genset. Responsible for Pier A to Nissan to Manuel. Have seen at Toyota at 1530.)

BNSF Interchange   Daily
> (On duty in the AM. Hauls cars between PHL and BNSF's Watson Yard. Runs in the street up the McFarland Lead when heading to Watson. Takes Rolling Junction to the Wilmington Lead when returning. Generally seems to have two four-axle units for power. Can run twice a day if needed.)

Dock Jobs (ten intermodal switch jobs)   Daily
> (On duty throughout the day – ten jobs or so. Identified by their call time and client. Two are the "7AM UP Dock Job" and "10AM BNSF Dock Job." Seems like a few of them leave about 0800. At 1500-1600 a number of jobs return to A Yard. All of these jobs report to UP and BNSF trainmasters and do anything from yarding full trains to switching at both yards and terminals. Also build and air-test outbound trains. They run all over Wilmington, Long Beach, Terminal Island, and Carson. They are on a fairly regular schedule, but at the disposal of the railroads. The weekly switching includes 50 starts split nearly evenly between UP and BNSF. UP trains include those to APL, TICTF, and ITS. BNSF trains include those to APM, PCT, WBCTF, and ITS. Also serve LBCT and Hanjin. All of these generally run with a single six-axle unit, but can have two.)

Long Beach Job   Mon-Fri
(On duty in the late afternoon – spot and pull from Toyota at Pier B, then work Pier D/Pier E spots under Gerald Desmond Bridge. Responsible for Pier A to TI to Toyota to Long Beach shippers Baker, GP Gypsum, and National Gypsum.)

Pasha Slab   As needed?
(On duty time unknown. Builds empty slab trains and switches loaded slab trains at Berths 177-173.)

UP Interchange   Mon-Fri
(On duty in the morning, maybe. Hauls cars between PHL and UP's Mead Yard (?). Use to run to Dolores (?). Seems to be a morning job.)

Terminal Jobs

GGS Switcher   Unknown
(In-terminal PHL contract switcher at Global Gateway South terminal switches the American President Lines there on west end of Terminal Island only. More often than not, uses one of the 3GS21Cs, although these are reported on the way out.)

Hanjin Switcher   Unknown
(In-terminal PHL contract switcher. Works Hanjin facility on Terminal Island. Kept in Hanjin switcher pocket when not working. Not visible from public areas.)

ITS Switcher   Unknown
(In-terminal PHL contract switcher, works fenced in International Transportation Service for K-Line in Long Beach, on north end of Pier J.)

LBCT Switcher   Unknown
(In-terminal PHL contract switcher, works fenced in Long Beach Container Terminal for OOCL in Long Beach, west of Pier G Yard.)

TICTF Switcher   Unknown
(In-terminal PHL contract switcher, works fenced in Terminal Island Container Transfer Facility for NYK/Evergreen on north end of Terminal Island.)

MedShipping Switcher   Unknown
(In-terminal PHL contract switcher. Switches Mediterranean south of Mead Yard.)

PCT Switcher   Unknown
(In-terminal PHL contract switcher, works fenced in Pacific Container Terminal for China Overseas in Long Beach, on south end of Pier J.)

WBCT Switcher   Unknown
(In-terminal PHL contract switcher. Works Yang Ming along West Basin. Power sits at Knoll when not in Yang Ming facility. Seems to have two runs, morning and afternoon.)

Rail America

(For all intents and purposes, Arizona & California and San Joaquin Valley are beyond the scope of this book. They are included as a bonus.)

Arizona & California (Cadiz)   Sun-Fri

(Cadiz Wye -Cadiz, CA – can view and photograph easily, no yard there, just the meet.)

(Trains arrive at Parker mid to late morning. Depart for Cadiz at 1200 because the BNSF Cadiz turn heads out at that time too. ACRZ takes approximately 3 1/2 hours running time to get to Cadiz. Occasionally has work on the way to Cadiz. The return run to Parker has been seen leaving as late as 1630. Entire run is on the old ATSF Parker subdivision. Both directions are called the "Cadiz Turn," but are also known by the ATSF job symbols, 708 westbound and 807 eastbound)

Ventura County (Oxnard)   As needed

(Ventura Country Railway – 301 Driffill Boulevard, Oxnard, CA – trucks park causing a limited and obstructed view of engine house. Useful to see if power is stashed, but not for photographs. Freight yard to the east is not accessible.)

(On duty approx 0930. Run as needed, working most weekdays. Move autoracks for Mazda on the Patterson Branch to and from Port Hueneme Naval base. Also work industries in south Oxnard and Port Hueneme industrial areas on the South Oxnard Branch, the Diamond Branch and the Edison Branch including Willamette Industries, MI Drilling, Halaco, Pacific Vehicle Processors, BMW, and Cook Composites. Return to Oxnard in late afternoon. Have a GP7u and an SW1200, but lately only use their Cal Northern GP15-1, which has RCL.)

San Diego & Imperial Valley (San Diego)   Mon-Fri

(MDTB Yard – Harbor Blvd south of Petco Park, San Diego, CA – nice afternoon view from ramp.)

(San Ysidro – 3003 East Beyer Boulevard, San Diego, CA – no legal access.)

(On duty 2330. Runs after San Diego Trolley finishes for the night. Works San Diego Trolley Blue Line south of MDTB Yard, making set outs and pickups down to San Ysidro. Also heads up the San Diego Trolley Orange Line to El Cajon to serve the local industries there. Brings cars back from San Ysidro and arrives in their yard about 0330. They will sometimes move them over to BNSF immediately and work there for an hour or more and tie up about 0430, depends on when they need to interchange. The SDIY power is left wherever they worked last, but some can usually be found at MDTB Yard. On most weeknights, jobs tie up at San Diego and San Ysidro. If they run to El Cajon, there isn't usually time to run back to San Diego so the crew will tie up in El Cajon, leaving MDTB yard empty. Have GP38-2s, GP40W-2Ls, and 3GS21Bs.)

San Joaquin Valley Railroad (Bakersfield, Fresno, and Exeter)

San Joaquin Valley will take UP symbols when running on UP. The LSxxxJ is a Union Pacific symbol. L for local, S probably for SJVR, and J for foreign railroad. The first digit is the terminal/crew base: 9 for Bakersfield, 8 for Goshen, and 6 and 7 for Fresno and Exeter (not sure which is which). The second and third digits represent the hour the crew went on-duty. For example the job based out of Goshen on-duty at 1500 hours would be the LS815J.

Goshen Job   Mon-Fri
(On duty in the morning at Exeter, works to Goshen Jct. alongside Goshen Blvd through Visalia. Transfers loads and empties between the two. Interchange with the UP is right off US 99 at Goshen. They switch the industrial park to the east of there. Runs westbound in the morning and eastbound in the afternoon/evening. Light is good on the mile of north-south running between Billy Goat Jct. and Visalia. There are twelve blocks of street running on Oak Ave. in Visalia proper.)

Lemoore Job   Mon-Fri
(On duty at 0800 and works west to Lemoore or Huron and returns working east to Goshen to interchange cars with the UP. The locomotive is kept in Lemoore near Leprino Foods' eastern-most cheese plant in downtown.)

Fresno Turn   Mon-Fri
(On duty mid-afternoon, transfers loads and empties to Fresno serving the shippers between Exeter and Fresno returning with cars from the Calwa Yard. Their locomotive is kept at Exeter. UP's LRF80 local delivers cars at Goshen to both the grain mill and SJVR.)

Fresno Job   Tue-Thu
(On duty in the morning, the former Fresno Interurban (Cameo Industrial lead) is worked from Fresno east to the industrial park near the airport on Tuesday and sometimes Thursday mornings.

Westside Job   Mon-Fri
(On duty time unknown. Works the former SP Westside line out of Fresno toward Firebaugh and
the former SP Riverdale Branch on other days. May no longer be daily.)

Bakersfield Switcher   Tue-Sat
(On duty 0400. Switches the SJVR cars at the BNSF yard. Then serves San Joaquin Petroleum and
Coast Petroleum on the Landco Sub. Power is kept at west end of BNSF yard.)

Oil Junction/Oil City Job   Mon-Fri
(On duty 0600. Heads to the refinery up the Oil City Subdivision – might be same job as
Bakersfield Switcher now. Have seen heading out of UP's Bakersfield Yard in the late morning.)

Buttonwillow Local   Mon-Fri
(Runs at night. Goes to Kern Oil & Refining plant in Harpertown on the Arvin Branch if there is
work. There are two customers on the Arvin, reefers of carrots from Bolthouse Farms in Algoso,
just 0.3 miles from Magunden, and Kern Oil & Refining. On the other branches, there are car
loadings at Buttonwillow and Rogas, as well as the Bakersfield industrial area from Kern Junction
to Gosford.)

Bakersfield Turn   Sun-Thu
(On duty 1500 hours on Sunday through Thursday the hauler transfers cars between the BNSF
and UP Yards. In addition the hauler also serves some of the shippers near Bakersfield on the
Arvin and the Buttonwillow Subs.)

Famoso Job   Mon-Fri
(On duty 1600. Runs to Famoso and switches the last two customers on the southern end of the
ATSF Porterville Sub; one at Hollis, the other near Famoso. Also switches a couple customers
near Lerdo and Cawelo. One of them is the rather large roofing shingle plant at Lerdo. Not
certain if this job still exists.)

The Sunset   Mon-Fri
(On duty 0830. The power for the Sunset is kept at Gosford. Arrives at Gulf near the I-5 Bridge at
about 1300 or so. Only go out to Levee once or twice a week. Conflicting reports of whether
they run a second evening job or not. Can work on Sat or Sun if there is need.)

Rogas Inergy Switcher   Unknown
(Inergy has a 6 stub tracks yard at Rogas, CA. They lease power from SJVR. Facility is not
accessible, and Inergy does the switching themselves. Not clear when they switch.)

Watco (Palouse River & Coulee City and Pacific Sun)

Pacific Sun – San Diego

(Stuart Mesa Yard – Camp Pendleton along the I-5 in Oceanside, CA. No legal access, however you can see if the power is tied up in the yard from the freeway.)

Escondido Local   Sun, Tue, Thu
(On duty 2000. Aren't usually moving until 2100. Starts from yard at Stuart Mesa, near the I-5. Heads up to Oceanside to make pickups and set outs, then heads up Escondido Branch to the end of track. They cannot enter the Escondido subdivision until the last eastbound Sprinter leaves the main track at Escondido about 2140. They do occasionally leave an extra engine at Escondido to assist with heavy switching.)

Miramar Local   Mon, Wed
(On duty 2000. Makes pick up and set-out at Oceanside. They then run down the coast to Miramar Industrial Spur if needed or up to San Onofre. Customers include the following commodities; corn, soy, lumber, plastic pellets, beer, paints and items for recycling. Have run extras to Miramar on Sunday afternoons when there is extra traffic.)

Ventura Foods – Ontario   As Needed

(Ventura Foods – East Mission Boulevard, Ontario, CA, west of Metrolink. Can see cars from street, but not the SW1500, unless it is running. Then clear shots.)

(Palouse River and Coulee City Railroad works in the evenings. Ventura leases a fleet of 180 tank cars. Their facility capacity in Ontario, including leads, is 106 cars over two spot tracks, one storage track, a storage lead, and a switching lead. PCC crews spot up to ten cars per day. Use an ex SOU, WAMX SW1500 that is parked deep inside the plant property when not on duty.)

TXI Riverside Cement– Oro Grande   Mon-Fri

(TXI Riverside – National Trails Highway, Oro Grande, CA. Can often see power from street. Facility cannot be accessed.)

(Palouse River and Coulee City Railroad operates on weekdays. Much of the switching can be seen from the shoulder of Route 66. Trains are run under contract. Have a Watco and a TXI GP35. When not working, units are parked separately and sometimes out of view. PM shots are possible if units have been left visible from street.)

US Military

Naval Weapons Station – Seal Beach   Suspended

(Being dismantled – not visible from public property. Locomotives, GE 80 tonners, do get randomly started and pulled out of engine house – Navy does not allow visitors – might display at a future open house events – but probably without cars, as engineers are all retired.)

Naval Base Ventura County – Port Hueneme   Suspended

(GE 80 tonner is dead in the marshaling yard. Hasn't been started since 2007. There is no way to reactivate it by Navy rules that require new engineers be trained by experienced engineers. Ventura County Railroad now provides limited switching when the base needs it.)

Marine Corps Base Camp Pendleton – Oceanside   Suspended?

(Switching services have been turned over to an unknown private operator. Marines have a low-nose ex SP GP9 which is parked at Fallbrook Junction, but is to be moved to PSRM soon. Little track exists beyond the wye itself, and currently there are no warehouses, fuel storage areas, vehicle loading ramps, or anything else directly served by the base railway. The railroad through the base has been dismantled with the exception of a three mile section extending from the old ranch house to the east border of the Marine base.)

Yermo Marine Corp Supply Center – Barstow (Nebo)   Unknown

(Looks like GE critters are viewable from A Street, of National Trails Highway.)

Yermo Marine Corp Supply Center – Yermo   Unknown

(Power is kept on the base, far from public view. Would need to get permission to enter the property. The base is served by UP just east of Barstow and has a large rail yard. There are two major inbound trains monthly from other military installations; much of it from Ft. Hood in Texas. Inbounds are set on the USMC spur by UP and the military switcher comes off-base to retrieve it. There are multiple locomotives, two 120 ton Army switchers, two Marine switchers - a 100 ton and an 80 ton, a couple GP10s, and a SW8. Most rail traffic is hidden on the base.)

Independent Short Lines

Fillmore & Western

(Fillmore & Western – Santa Clara Avenue, Fillmore, CA. Can see most power from the street and some will usually be parked where it can be photographed, but cannot access yard.)

Passenger Trains   Sat-Sun and some weekday
> (Run excursion trains from Fillmore to Santa Paula, with extremely infrequent service to Piru also. Passenger train schedules are fairly extensive and can be found on their website, www.fwry.com. Have an RS32, two GP35s, an S6, two F7s, a Consolidation, and a steam industrial engine. Also have three derelict S6s in yard.)

Freight Trains   As needed
> (Perform rare freight deliveries, picking up a car from Santa Paula and delivering to a customer in Fillmore. Will take extra locomotive to Santa Paula on a passenger train and then leave it behind to pick up the freight. Bridge in Saticoy is presently out of service though.)

Movie Trains   As needed
> (Can run anytime and be anything, included importing power.)

Santa Maria Valley

(Spreckles Factory – West Betteravia Road, Santa Maria, CA. Can shoot from street if power is there.)

Town Job – Santa Maria   Mon-Fri
> (On duty about 1000 most days, but can start as late as 1400. Run weekdays from an old sugar plant in Betteravia to Guadalupe and into Santa Maria, switching customers along the way. Much of the line is not accessible and some branches are used for car storage. Use GP9 for heavy trains and 70t for light trains. GP9 is usually at "Freezer" while 70t is more likely at Betteravia. RR is railfan friendly as long as you don't trespass. Most work on Mondays and Thursdays is pulling empties. Most work on Tuesdays and Fridays is delivering loads.)

Carrizo Gorge   Very rare

(Carrizo Gorge – North end of Railroad Street, Jacumba, CA. Power can be seen and photographed from public areas, but may be obstructed.)

> (Railroad is presently embargoed, although a new owner is reportedly trying to reactivate at least some of it. Makes rare movements to move stored cars. Most equipment is in Jacumba, including a GP40, GP9, F7s, and an S4.)

Baja California Rail Road, Inc.

Freight   Mon-Fri

> (On duty 0600. Use two GP38s leased from Larry's Truck & Electric. These locomotives are LTEX 3808 and LTEX 3809. They are former Santa Fe units in the yellow and blue "Blue Bonnet" scheme. Power is kept at the Tijuana depot house track. A US crew brings empties from Tijuana to San Ysidro, CA for the SDIY interchange then shuttles loads back to Tijuana. Leave San Ysidro by 1000. A Mexican crew takes over for the run to Garcia every day, to Redondo 4x a week and to Tecate 3x a week. There is no service east of Tecate.)

Passenger   Monthly on a Saturday

> (On duty 0800. Departs Garcia 0900. Runs once a month on Saturdays. Runs from Garcia to Tecate. CZRY BAJA operated the train and the last scheduled run on the website was in 2011— http://www.fcbc.com.mx/anuncio_tttt.htm. Might be done for.)

Plaster City Railroad – US Gypsum   Mon-Fri

(US Gypsum – County Highway 80, Plaster City, CA. If power is in can see and photograph from street.)

> (Crew is on duty at 0800. On the move north 0900. Return to Plaster City late afternoon, early evening. Does not work weekends. Make one or two runs a day from Plaster City to mine as needed. The quarry is located in the Fish Creek Mountains of Imperial County and is estimated to contain a deposit of 25 million tons of gypsum. RR won't run if plant is slow. Railfan friendly if you check in at US Gypsum office first.)

Southern California Railroad   As needed

(US Gypsum – County Highway 80, Plaster City, CA. Power is kept inside. Cannot access, Cannot see unless running.)

> (Does the standard gauge switching under contract for USG at Plaster City. Used to switch three times a week. But is now an as needed operation, and can work as little as once a week. Have a GP9 and a GP40. Power is parked within the plant. RR is part of American Railroads Corp.)

Mojave Northern Railroad – Cemex   Maybe daily

(Cemex Victorville – 16463 National Trails Highway, Victorville, CA. Some good views from street, but power can be obstructed.)

(Inbound leaves the mine, which is 12 miles northeast of Victorville, at about 0600, outbound leaves the plant about 0900, second inbound about 1345, second outbound about 1615. Train shuttles loads of pulverized calcium carbonate. Have an SD60, SD40-2, two GP39-2s, an SWP SDP35 and a Shuttlewagon. Coal comes in off the UP. Cement goes out on BNSF or UP. Guard shack was recently erected blocking much of the parallel road.)

Trona Railroad   Mon-Sat as needed

(Trona – Mountain View and Main, Trona, CA. There is no yard access and there is very heavy security.)

(Often on duty 1600, but runs as needed. Will run most days Mon-Sat. Do not run on Sundays. They usually switch the yards in the morning and send a train to Searles in the afternoon/evening for a headlight meet with UP. It's tough to know exactly when because they call the UP that day or the day before and ask when they are going to get to Searles and time the meet accordingly. There's not much to see in the yards but there are some nice photo spots out along the 32 mile line. The whole turn takes about 4-5 hours. Power is ex UP SD40-2s and ex SP SD40T-2s still in their old paint. Have an SD9 for switching. Railroad is owned by Searles Valley Minerals. They carry sulfuric acid, soda ash, potash, salt cake, Borax, coal, minerals, and material for the U.S. Navy China Lake Facility. Finish up between 1830 and 2030.)

Industrial Switchers

British Petroleum – Carson   Mon-Fri

(On duty 0600 Mon-Fri. They have an SW9 hidden deep in the refinery. There is an SW1200 visible from the Sepulveda overpass. It pulls from the refinery to Dolores, and can be photographed from Alameda, but it's a long telephoto shot. They also have an SP low-nose GP9E that is left at the butane LPG racks in the yard along the industrial road off 223rd Street and reportedly belongs to Inter-Rail Group. The only grade crossing is just east of the LPG racks on the industrial road off 223rd and hypothetically any of the three could be photographed when passing over it. The entire RR shuts down by 1300. Employees will tell you photography is illegal. Don't trespass unless you want to be arrested.)

PolyOne – Carson   Mon-Fri

(On duty 0900 Mon-Fri. as needed, done around 1300. Unit can be shot with a telephoto in the summer from the fence on 223rd, but it's not a great shot. When working it will cross the service road off on 223rd Street between 1000 to 1300. Faces west and is almost always front coupled. Plant makes thermoplastic resins. Guards will not allow you on the property.)

Pacific Railroad Society – Commerce   Rare Sa or Su

(Pacific Railroad Society has a GE 45t that they occasionally use to move cars at their yard in on Naokes near Herbert in Commerce, north of the east end of Union Pacific's East Yard. Can be seen from street, but there is no photo possible.)

Chevron – El Segundo (Savage)   Mon-Fri

(On duty 1700/1800, but can start later. Ends its day by 0500. Work in the property first. They head over the only legal place to watch them, the grade crossing on Sepulveda after 0000. Once east of Sepulveda, they grab cars from UP and BNSF and then shove them back into the refinery, where they switch them out. Their engine house is deep in the facility. Trains are crewed by Savage and have a low nosed Geep and a genset on the property. Occasionally they will leave a unit in the yard east of Sepulveda for Union Pacific to haul out for servicing or rotation.)

Metro Ports – Long Beach   As Needed

(Run as needed to transload ships, either white aggregates or coal. Also shove loaded trains into Pier G Yard. Generally use the genset to transload and the SF30C to shove loaded trains; however the genset is the main power. When they park a unit at the aggregate loader it can be seen, and shot, from the fence along the northwestern part of their property. The genset faces north and the U-Boat faces south.)

BP Coke – Wilmington Calciner – Wilmington   As needed

(Have a nicely kept SW9 on a track that runs alongside the parking lot and right up to near the front gate fence. It faces north and is a good summer morning shot, but is obstructed by the fence just before the guard gate. The plant produces calcinized coke to make carbon anodes for the aluminum industry.)

GATX Colton Service Center – Colton   Mon-Fri

(Run 0720 to at least 1500, with a lunch break . MP14B can be shot from Pepper with a telephoto lens. The best sun is in winter afternoons. There are also three critters on property, all dead, one plinthed. The facility cleans and service GATX fleet cars and always has a tremendous amount of cars coming in.)

California Steel Industries – Fontana   Mon-Fri

(There are at least three jobs on weekday mornings using one SW900 and three SW1500s. At least one job works Sat mornings. Often see a job working in the late afternoon early evening too. Only public view is from San Bernardino Ave – but seems like most jobs pass by there if you wait long enough. The best view is across from Staub Metals and the scale tower. The engine house is deep on property, way out of view.)

George Verhoeven Grain – Ontario   Mon-Fri

(Seems to work in the morning. They have a former Arizona & California GP30 still in green and cream that can be seen from the Etiwanda overpass. It is much too far to photograph from there. Sometimes the unit works east and can be seen from Airport Road. Probably a good shot from parking lot when this happens, but would need permission to be on their property.)

General Motors Distribution Center– San Bernardino   As Needed

(Inter-Rail Group works when there are autoracks to unload or load, never leaving the yard. Switch crew makes sure everything is on spot and builds the outbound trains. The have two chop-nosed Transitank TANX GP7s and an ex BN and BNSF SD40-2. The facility is carved out of the east side of BNSF's B-Yard. Only possible shot is telephoto through a tight mesh fence.)

Cargill – Verdemont   Unknown

(They have a remote control GP9 that was normally parked right out in the open along the BNSF Cajon Sub south of Devore. It's a good late afternoon shot. RCL operation. Recently got a Western Rail SD40T-2. Not clear if this is in addition or as a replacement.)

US Borax Boron Mine – Boron   As Needed

(Has no particular schedule. If busy, all three units, a GP39-2, a SW1, and a GP9, can be running at the same time. To access Rich Spur take the dirt road that trucks use for the loading plant. There is an area there where you can safely park and watch the switchers work.)

Speckles Sugar – Brawley   Suspended?

(Was Holly Sugar. There is a DM20 and a 25t visible from Google Earth, but on the far side of plant, where you can't see them from street. It appears that RR operations may be shut down. Can't see their Trackmobile anywhere. Would need to get permission to visit first.)

Mitsubishi Cement Cushenbury Plant – Lucerne Valley   Unknown

(Have an old Plymouth MDT hidden very deep within the plant. It can only be seen on plant tours, although it's not actually a part of the tour itself. Would probably have to ask the tour guide for a special side trip.)

Niklor Chemical – Mojave   Unknown

(On Purdy Avenue, south of Mojave, east of Route 14. They have an S1M, de-cabbed rebuild, called a "Bug Slug" that appears to be behind a fence at all times. Employees are reportedly railfan friendly. Google shows the unit off a private road east of the facility.)

Progress Rail Services – Mojave   Unknown

(On the south end of Roper Road in Mojave Airport. They have an SW9, which is unlettered. The unit sits out in the open, and is usually easy to photograph, if not parked behind something. No idea when it works. Had a Trackmobile too, but it may be gone. The company does work on rail wheels.)

Celite – White Hills   Unknown

(South of Lompoc, CA on UP's White Hills Industrial Lead. All switching is done within the property of World Minerals and not visible from public locations. They use an ex SOU SW1500 painted "Celite" but with reporting marks NREX. This unit gets serviced at Betteravia when needed. World Minerals also operates narrow-gauge mining tram motors deep in the plant. They mill diatomaceous earth, used in toothpaste, beer filtering, and swimming pool filters.)

Imperial Irrigation Dam – Winterhaven   Unknown

(At the top of County Road 24. They have a Brookville BSA and train that sit out in the open… They are used to transport refuse from dam filters. PM shot.)

Rail Tractor Operations

Union Pacific – Bloomington   Trackmobile
    (West Colton engine house switcher.)

Speckles Sugar – Brawley   Trackmobile
    (See in industrials)

Kinder Morgan – Carson   Trackmobile and Shuttlewagon SWX605C
    (Can only see when working – kept deep on property – KM employees do not like photographers
    and will come after you even if you photograph from public location. Was actually chased down
    the street by one who then sent LASD to my house.)

Ventura Transfer – Carson   Rail King RK285
    (Runs in the morning – Mon-Fri – with what appears to be two different Rail Kings, they cross
    the industrial road that swings off 223rd Street in order to work the two yards. Yard to the east
    was once part of Arco. This is a heavily guarded industrial area with refineries, so be smart and
    careful.)

Shell Oil – Carson   Trackmobile
    (Del Amo & Wilmington – have a large Trackmobile on the facility, cannot be seen from street.)

CalPortland Cement – Colton   Shuttlewagon
    (Large Shuttlewagon looks more like a red locomotive from Google Earth. Right along Cement
    Plant Road, but beyond guard gate. Would need permission. Afternoon shot.)

Pacific Rail Industries – Colton   Shuttlewagon SWX525B
    (Shifts aggregate hoppers in Old Colton Yard at M and Mount Vernon. Can only be seen from
    street when it is on the east side of their transloading facility.)

Western Milling – Colton   Trackmobile
    (Large grain elevator at Ice Deck. Have at least one Trackmobile to move cars.)

Timco Steel (TST Inc) – Fontana   Trackmobile
    (On Etiwanda, south of Jurupa… little yellow Trackmobile appears to be visible from the street,
    just inside the gate – would be a PM shot.)

Triumph Aerostructures – Hawthorne   Trackmobiles
    (Just south of Hawthorne Airport. Have two Trackmobiles to shuttle the cars around and spot
    near the fence when ready to go. No way to see from street as always on north end of cars.)

K-Line – Long Beach   Trackmobile 5500 TM & Shuttlewagon SWX605Be
    (At ITS. Visible from north side of annual Green Port Long Beach Metrolink train. Makes a few
    moves around the facility but PHL does all train spotting and building.)

Amtrak—Los Angeles   Shuttlewagon
(Have a Shuttlewagon at Redondo roundhouse for quick moves of coaches. Usually parked visible from Santa Fe.)

Cereal Food Processors – Los Angeles   one or two Trackmobiles
(Can be seen north of the corner of 1861 East 55th Street and Alameda. When there are hoppers on the property. Would be a morning shot, but there is a fence and machine seems to be stored inside.)

Polychemie – Los Angeles   unknown
(Have a rail tractor that they use in their East LA facility on the end of the Mojave Granite Spur near Alhambra. Pushes tank cars from Miller Ave to under the Soto Street Bridge in the morning. UP YZ71R then picks up cars. The author has NO visual confirmation of this machine)

CalPro/TTX – Mira Loma   unknown
(Have a Trackmobile looking device that they use to move cars around the CalPro facility that still receives bad order cars.)

California Portland Cement – Mojave   Shuttlewagon
(Appears to be a Shuttlewagon at the Creal plant at the end of the Oak Creek Lead. Shuttlewagon is past the gate and does not appear accessible.)

Progress Rail Service – Mojave   Rail King
(See industrials.)

Portland Cement – Monolith   Rail King RK275
(Can see the Rail King RK275 from the street. Reportedly have a second machine also.)

TXI Riverside Cement – National City   two Trackmobiles
(Looks like you can drive in and photograph, PM shot, kept off the track, 920 Bay Marina Drive.)

Praxair – Ontario   Trackmobile
(Deep in the property at 5621 East Airport Drive, Ontario. Would need permission.)

International Paper – Oxnard   Shuttlewagon SWX315
(Can see from street, but there is a guard right there and parking is not possible. At southern end of Perkins. This plant has been closed. Not sure what the future will bring.)

Paramount Petroleum – Paramount   Trackmobile
(Square yellow Trackmobile, kept on the Pacific Electric Santa Ana line, but behind the refinery fence. Cannot see from street.)

Metropolitan Water District chlorine station – Perris   Shuttlewagon
(On Patterson, at end of Granite Spur, off wye south of Val Verde from the San Jac Industrial Spur. Shuttlewagon is deep on property. Facility has been closed. Not sure what is used for now.)

Star Milling – Perris   Trackmobile
(On Water Street at BNSF ROW. Small white tractor, looks like visible from ROW, may be visible from parking lot.)

Honeyville Grain – Rancho Cucamonga   Trackmobile 4160 TM
(Sitting at track on west end of parking lot. Looks like you can just drive in and photograph it. East of Milliken at Pasadena Sub.)

Tamco – Rancho Cucamonga   Rail King
(Might be two of them, both kept very deep on property – cannot see from street. West of Etiwanda at Pasadena Sub.)

Boise Building Supplies – Riverside   Trackmobile
(Near end of Ruhr Spur, sits near fence. Not visible from street, just a bit up the track.)

A&R Transport Inc – San Bernardino   Rail King RK320
(Rail King at Rancho and Toranga, by BNSF B- Yard. Works midday. Can be shot from the sidewalk, northeast of the facility, if the Rail King is coming to the throat of the yard.)

Greenbrier Railroad Services – San Bernardino   Shuttlewagon?
(At end of Cooley Court, along Redlands Branch ROW. Doesn't look accessible from street, maybe from ROW. Long walk west from Tippecanoe.)

American President Lines – San Pedro   Trackmobile?
(Used in Global Gateway… not sure where kept. Makes a few moves around the facility but PHL does all train spotting and building.)

Air Liquide America – Santa Fe Springs   Trackmobile
(At Dice and the UP tracks, have one blue, small Trackmobile on the northeast end of their spur where it is deep on their property and impossible to see from the street.)

CTS Cement Manufacturing – Santa Fe Springs   Trackmobile
(At Marquardt and Firestone in SFS, bulk transloading facility. Machine is parked in the middle of fenced in parking lot, but if yard is empty can be shot from ROW.)

Maersk – San Pedro (Terminal Island)   Trackmobile?
(Pier 400, not sure where kept. Makes a few moves around the facility but BNSF does all train spotting and building.)

Vopak – San Pedro (Terminal Island)   Trackmobile
(On Old Dock Street, just under the Henry Ford Bridge, only UP customer on the island. Trackmobile appears to be parked off the tracks.)

Tecate Beer – Tecate, BC   Mercedes rail tractor
(Hard to see from street, behind wall usually. Would have to get permission.)

Exxon Mobil Refinery – Torrance   Trackmobile
(Small blue tractor looking Trackmobile, deep inside fence cannot be seen from road.)

General Mills – Vernon   Shuttlewagon SWX435 and Rail King RK330
  (One is usually parked on east end of mill, viewable at street through fence.)

Cemex – Victorville   Shuttlewagon SWX525
  (Plant switcher alongside Rte 66.)

Conoco Phillips – Wilmington   Trackmobile
  (Have large Trackmobile in the former Tosco refinery alongside I-110. Cannot be accessed
  without permission.)

Pacific Harbor Line – Wilmington   Trackmobile
  (Inside Pier A Yard… not clear what it is used for.)

Places where Parked Power Is Photographable

Anaheim, UP – 1599 W. Mable Street, Anaheim (Any time)

Buena Park, UP – 6498 Regio Avenue, Buena Park (AM)

Commerce, BNSF – 6258 East 26th Street, Commerce (usually blocked by freight cars, sometimes open)

Commerce, UP – 3652 East Washington Boulevard, Commerce (AM, parking is not possible)

Corona, BNSF – 327 Radio Road, Corona (AM – can be parked too far back to see)

Fontana, BNSF -8815 Cherry Avenue, Fontana (PM – can photograph from bridge or access road)

La Mirada, BNSF – 14569 Macaw Street, La Mirada (PM – low fence is in way... annoying)

Lancaster, Metrolink – 44812 N. Sierra Highway, Lancaster (Summer AM or PM shot, but fence in way)

Los Angeles, Amtrak – Olympic Blvd at Los Angeles River (shoot down at 8th Street)

Mira Loma, UP – Western end of 8th Street in the Space Center north of the yard (PM shot in winter)

Moorpark, Metrolink – 258 Poindexter Avenue, Moorpark (PM, photographing over fence – not good)

Oceanside, Metrolink -Carmelo Drive, Oceanside (AM shot)

Oxnard, UP – 319 E. 5th St, Oxnard (PM shot, can be blocked if yard is loaded, need a telephoto)

Oxnard, VCRR – 301 Driffill Boulevard, Oxnard (photographing over fence, bad angles – not worth it)

Riverside, Metrolink -4066 Vine Street, Riverside (Very tight, fences, so not good, but can see and shoot power if one wants)

San Bernardino, Metrolink – 1204 West 3rd Street, San Bernardino (Nice open AM shot)

San Luis Obispo, UP - 1011 Railroad Avenue, San Luis Obispo (Afternoon shot of pushers)

Santa Fe Spring, UP – 11407 Los Nietos Road, SFS (PM – gate can be closed, then photographing through fence)

Ventura, Metrolink – 6301 Nightingale Street, Ventura (face the wrong way... cab cars face open space)

Whittier, UP – 9131 Santa Fe Springs Road (AM)

Wilmington, BNSF -1301 Lomita Blvd. Tie up track is along Lomita.

Plinthed Power

Bakersfield, Kern County Museum – Chester & 38th – SP Mastodon 4-8-0 - (faces east, fence on south side)

Barstow, Western American RR Museum – FP45, SD40-2, 44t, Beep (face both ways)

Colton, GATX – 20878 Slover St – Plymouth JLB-2 (faces south, behind fence – need tele)

La Mesa, PSRM – Lemon & Nebo – MNRR 0-6-0 (faces south, fence on east side)

Loma Linda, Heritage Park – 15513 Mosher Avenue, Alco S4 (faces east, behind fence)

Lomita, Lomita Railroad Museum – 250th Street – SP 2-6-0 (faces south, fence)

Los Angeles, CA, Nat History Museum – 900 Exposition Boulevard – PE Sand Car (indoors)

Lytle Creek, CA, Green Mountain Ranch – three Plymouths (face east and north, one altered)

Mexicali, Mexico – Sol del Niño Museum near downtown – Hi Nose FSBC GP40

Mexicali, Mexico – city park near the S-BC Depot, FC Sonora Baja GR-32   2-8-0

Mexicali, Mexico – Milepost 49B on Ferromex – SP M 2-6-0

Newhall, William Hart Ranch – 24151 Newhall Avenue – SP 2-6-0 (faces north – obstructed)

Ontario – Euclid and B Street – Ontario and San Antonio horse car (in building, bad photo)

Oceanside, Pendleton Museum – Vandergrift Blvd & Rattlesnake Cyn – GE 80t (faces SW)

Redlands, San Bernardino Museum – 2024 Orange Tree Lane – SP 2-8-0 (faces east, fence)

Riverside, Fairmount Park – Bowling Green & Fairmount – UP 2-8-0 (faces east, fence)

San Diego, Museum of San Diego History – 1649 El Prado, Balboa Park – trolley (pics not allowed)

Santa Fe Springs, Heritage Park, 12100 Mora Drive – ATSF 2-8-0 (faces northeast, open)

Santa Maria, CA, by old engine house – Union Sugar 0-4-0T

Seal Beach, Electric Avenue Park – Electric & Main – PE Line Car (faces southeast, lots of trees)

Sylmar, Nethercutt Collection – 15151 Bledsoe Street – CP 4-6-4 (facing southwest)

Torrance, Wilson Park – 2283 Washington Avenue – PE Blimp (cut in half, faces west, fence)

Tustin, Weber Plywood – 15513 Mosher Avenue – Plymouth DL-2 (clear on Sun, faces northeast)

Railroad Museums & Tourist Railroads

Alpine, CA – **Descanso, Alpine & Pacific**   Sundays

(Small tourist railroad runs trains behind a 2 ½ ton Brookville. Run on Sundays from 1300 to 1500 by appointment.)

Anaheim, CA – **California Adventure Red Car**   Daily

(There are two replica Pacific Electric Big Red Cars that run in the park during normal park hours.)

Anaheim, CA – **Disneyland Railroad**   Daily

(Run between two and four steam trains at a time, utilizing a roster of five steam engines. All are rather whimsical, but still real locomotives. They also have a fleet of three very modern looking monorails. All trains run most of every day, but are hard to get unobstructed photos of.)

Buena Park, CA – **Knott's Berry Farm** - Ghost Town & Calico Railroad   Daily

(Have one train running nearly all times the park is open. Two Rio Grande narrow gauge Mikados alternate on heavy days. There is a Galloping Goose that takes over on light days. Crews are friendly and give cab rides when safe. There are also two other locomotives there on display, a logging saddle-tank and some sort of large amusement park engine.)

Campo, CA – **Pacific Southwest Railway Museum Association**   Sat-Sun

(Have excursion trains, but they do not run every open day. Have a roster of six steam engines and 15 diesels from almost every manufacturer including an AS616, RS2, H20-44, and some real oddballs. Not the entire roster is on display. Trains are run behind a GP9 or an 80t, but those are not the only locomotives that run. Very friendly volunteers and an excellent adventure.)

Fillmore, CA – **Fillmore & Western**   Sat-Sun +

(Have a recently restored steam engine and a great diesel roster. Run trains to Santa Paula and on rare occasion to Piru. There is more information on FWRR in shortlines section.)

Glendale, CA – **Americana at Brand**   Daily

(Gomaco trolley with trailer runs in a loop around a very upscale shopping center. Can be seen from one street, but mostly is inside the mall – guards unfriendly)

Industry, CA – **Pacific Palms Industry Hills Funicular**   Suspended

> (Funicular for golf carts runs from the main resort hotel up a hill. Trams are reportedly no longer in operation but still visible from the parking lot.)

Los Angeles, CA – **Angel's Flight**   Daily

> (Historic funicular in downtown Los Angeles to the top of Bunker Hill. Runs on a very frequent schedule during the day.)

Los Angeles, CA – **Getty Center**   Daily

> (Otis Hovair Shuttle, which is sort of a cross between a monorail and a sideways elevator, makes constant runs throughout the day. Each Hovair is a three-car train. They are easy to photograph from the walkway alongside the tracks.)

Los Angeles, CA – **The Grove**   Daily

> (A double-deck reproduction trolley makes the short run back and forth between the Grove Mall and Farmer's Market. Trolley won't run on extremely heavy mall-traffic days, or if there is an exhibit of any kind. Even when running, spends a lot of time recharging. There is a wigwag signal midway.)

Los Angeles, CA – **Travel Town**   Daily

> (Nice collection of steam, some electric, and diesels, including a PE Blimp and steeplecab, as well an RS12 and rare EMD Model 40. PM shots better)

National City, CA – **SDERA** San Diego Electric Railway Association   Sundays

> (Have three Austrian trams and an American Birney car at that ATSF depot. Very nice morning shots.)

Perris, CA – **Orange Empire Railway Museum**   Museum daily, Rides Sat-Sun

> (Have a huge streetcar, interurban, and diesel collection, with some steam too. This is the "too numerous to mention" museum in California. Their diesel collection includes just about every manufacturer possible.)

Pomona, CA – **RR & Loco Historical Society**   Second weekend of the month plus Fair Days

> (Fantastic collection of huge steam locomotives and a DD40X. Everything faces southeast.)

Poway, CA – **Poway-Midland Railway**   Weekends, limited

> (They run a gussied up 0-4-0T and LA streetcar on a small tourist railroad.)

San Diego, CA – **San Diego Vintage Trolley**   Tu, Th, Sa, Su

    (Silver line PCC car runs in downtown loop from 1100 to 1530. They are presently restoring more cars in San Diego Electric Railway colors.)

San Pedro, CA – **Port of Los Angeles Waterfront Red Car Line**   Fr, Sa, Su

    (Two replica PE cars and one real one alternate on this line, although the real one only gets used on special occasions. Cars run 1200-2130 in Summer and 1200-1700 in Winter.)

Santa Clarita, CA – **Six Flags Magic Mountain Funicular**   Daily

    (Have a European, mid-century style funicular inside the park called *Orient Express*. They also have an older, open car, monorail, but it is presently out of service, and not expected to come back.)

Passenger Railroads

Amtrak – (main yard 8th Street, Los Angeles)

Coaster (main yard Stuart Mesa)

Los Angeles Metro Rail (various light rail and subway – some guards are anti railfan)

Metrolink (yards in East Ventura, Moorpark, Lancaster, San Bernardino, Riverside, and Oceanside)

San Diego Trolley (main yard in downtown by Petco Park)

Sprinter (light rail, main yard Escondido)

Wig Wag Signals

Anaheim, CA – Lemon and Santa Anita (LOA31, LOA32)

Colton, CA – 9th and M (YWC80, YWC86)

Gardena, CA – Denker and 168th (LOW10)

Gardena, CA – Hobart and 168th (LOW10)

Hanford, CA – Brown Street between 5th and 6th (SJVR)

Hawthorne, CA – Eucalyptus and Broadway (LOW20)

Redlands, CA – Nevada and Industrial Park (Track out of service)

(Also – there are operating wigwags at the Orange Empire Museum in Perris, a faux wigwag at The Grove in Los Angeles, and many others on display at various museums.)

Restaurants and Bars Made Up of Railroad Cars

Acton – Vincent Hill Station Restaurant & Saloon (Sierra Highway) – restaurant/bar with a number of SP, ATSF, and UP cabooses in the back.

Anaheim – Stardust Motel (Ball and Disneyland) – two old Pullmans and two cabooses. Not much of a shot possible.

Barstow – McDonalds Barstow Stations (on Main Street, east of downtown) – six old passenger cars. Better afternoon shot.

Buellton – abandoned diner made up of two Los Angeles Transit Line trolley cars (on service road north of town). Sadly, has recently been torn down. Not sure if trolley bodies will be moved.

Oceano – Rock & Roll Café (Railroad Avenue) – have two old streamliner cars. Would be a morning shot, summer morning if you want to get light on the observation car end.

San Juan Capistrano – Sarducci's Capistrano Depot (at Amtrak station) - There are box cars and a caboose from an old Victoria Station theme restaurant.

Shafter – Red Wagon (Burbank and Beech) – diner made out of a Pacific Electric 500 car. Afternoon shot.

Studio City – Carneys (Ventura Blvd.) – hot dog stand made out of old UP passenger cars and ATSF caboose. Morning shot.

West Hollywood – Carneys (Sunset Blvd.) – hot dog stand made out of old UP passenger cars. Morning shot.

West Hollywood – Formosa Cafe (Formosa and Santa Monica) – bar is an old Pacific Electric 800 car, although the front of it has been altered, making it look like the back of the building. Afternoon shot.

Made in the USA
Las Vegas, NV
02 July 2024

91784148R00044